THE STORY OF WITCHES

WILLOW WINSHAM

THE STORY OF WITCHES

DEDICATED TO WITCHES EVERYWHERE – PAST, PRESENT AND FUTURE.

BATSFORD

Contents

Introduction:
The World of the Witch — 6

Part One:

From Hekate to Baba Yaga: Witches of Fairy Tale,
   Myth and Legend — 10
Goddess of Witches: The Many Faces of Hekate — 13
Double, Double, Toil and Trouble: The Witches of *Macbeth* — 17
From Dame Gothel to Hansel and Gretel:
   Witches in Folk and Fairy Tales — 21
The Witch with the Chicken-Legged Hut: Baba Yaga — 27
Milk Magic: Butter Stealing and Milk Thieves — 30
I Shall Go Into a Hare: The Hare and the Witch — 38
From Alewives to the Wicked Witch of the West:
   Why Do Witches Wear Pointed Hats? — 42
Perchta the Belly Slitter and other Midwinter Witches — 45

Part Two:

The Witch Among Us: The Witch Trials and Beyond — 56
Thou Shalt Not Suffer a Witch To Live — 59
The Hammer of Witches: *Malleus Maleficarum* — 61
Baby Fat and Sex with Satan: The Witches' Sabbath — 63
In the Devil's Name — 71

From Midsummer to Halloween: When Witches Meet	76
Taking to the Skies: Witches and Broomsticks	78
Pricking and Swimming: A Discovery of Witches	80
Imps and Demons: The Witch's Familiar	95
Protection and Charms: How to Foil a Witch	102
Scratch the Witch	105

Part Three:

The Witch Cult and Beyond: The Many Paths of the Witch Today	116
Margaret Murray and the Myth of the Witch Cult	119
The Advent of Wicca	121
Robert Cochrane and Traditional Witchcraft	126
The Mother of Modern Witchcraft: Doreen Valiente	129
King of the Witches: Alexandrian Wicca	132
Dianic Wicca	134
The Reclaiming Tradition: Starhawk and *The Spiral Dance*	137
Solitary Practitioners: The Way of the Hedge Witch	139
Maiden, Mother, Crone: The Great Goddess	141
From Cernunnos to the Green Man: The Horned God	144
The Wheel of the Year	148
Gerald Gardner and Operation Cone of Power	161
A Dark Heritage: Remembering Our Witches	165
Acknowledgements	176
Select Bibliography	178
Index	184

Introduction:
The World of the Witch

The witch – malevolent, magical, multi-faceted – has walked among us for centuries.

An integral and often deeply troubling feature of our shared human experience, it is rare indeed to find a nation or culture without some concept of the witch. In our stories and superstitions, our traditions and our very history, the witch has been with us: at times lurking in the shadows, at others thrust into the limelight, but always, inescapably, present.

In the most basic terms, the word 'witch' has historically been used to mean one who causes harm to others through evil magic. Like the very spells witches are said to wield, words have power, and 'witch' has been used in many ways: as a slur; a way to denigrate, control and coerce; as a weaponized label thrust upon countless individuals without their consent, to name but a few. The villain of many a story, real or imagined, the terrifying truth of the witch is that she is both one of us, yet not: she is human, but also far from it.

This book explores the ever-evolving image of and beliefs surrounding the witch. There have been countless valuable volumes written about all aspects of witchcraft history and folklore, and it would take many, many more words than are available here to cover the history of the witch in its entirety. Instead, the pages that follow delve into the key aspects of witches: how they were viewed, treated and written about, both by those on the outside and by the witches themselves.

From Hekate to Baba Yaga, from shape-shifting hares to the witches of *Macbeth*, Part One is a rich dive into the many ideas and depictions of witches across folklore, myth and legend, fairy tale and superstition. Part Two delves into the tumultuous and bloody period of the witch trials, exploring the lives of those involved and the beliefs and experiences that made up one of the darkest periods of our collective history. What exactly was the Witches' Sabbath? How did a witch bottle help identify a witch? Just how many people accused as witches lost their lives at the stake or gallows, and why? Part Three brings us through more recent times, looking in particular at how the image and identity of the witch has been reclaimed and reinvented, from the ideas of Margaret Murray and the witch cult, to the advent of Wicca and modern witchcraft and beyond.

Finally and most crucially comes the vital question: what have we learned from the past and what is the best way to approach our – often terrible – shared history of the witch?

Author's Note: Due to the inevitable constraints of word count and space, it is impossible to do justice to the full wealth of witch and witchcraft-related belief across the globe. Therefore, the decision has been taken to focus primarily on material from Europe and the USA.

PART ONE

From Hekate to Baba Yaga: Witches of Fairy Tale, Myth and Legend

Humankind has always loved to tell stories.
Before the written word, these stories were an essential mode of communication, an intrinsic necessity in order to pass on beliefs, traditions and warnings from one generation to the next. The first recorded fairy tale is believed to date back to 6,000 years ago, and it is clear that this is only the tip of the iceberg in our storytelling heritage.

Within this tradition of myths, legends and tales, witches have terrified, titillated and entertained us for millennia. Passed down by word of mouth and then on into the written record, tales of witches – powerful, cunning and often deadly – have held a timeless fascination for us. From the biblical Witch of Endor to the Arthurian Morgan Le Fay, from the

witch in Hansel and Gretel to Cinderella's Fairy Godmother, otherworldly, with supernatural powers and abilities, the witch plays many roles. A figure of fear, the end point of a quest, an enemy to overcome, a warning: again and again, the witch confronts us through our superstitions, fairy tales, cautionary tales and legends, holding up a mirror to us as individuals and humankind as a whole. From ancient goddesses to fairy-tale stepmothers, the witch has been presented in a variety of forms, the only constant being that she is never far away.

It is also through this shared body of tales that we come closest to knowing the people of the past; what our distant ancestors thought, believed, did and feared. Through them we can glimpse how witches were viewed and treated, and the part the witch played in the minds and lives of everyday people.

Goddess of Witches:
The Many Faces of Hekate

Of all the deities of the ancient world, none can rival the Greek goddess Hekate for her position as most associated with witches and witchcraft. The goddess of darkness and magic, sacrifices and crossroads, today Hekate is the very embodiment of the witch, capturing the imagination of academics, writers and members of the Neopagan community alike.

Considering her later reputation, Hekate's beginnings are surprisingly tame by comparison. The goddess's origins are not found in Ancient Greece at all, and it is believed that her roots lie in Caria, a region of what is now modern-day Turkey. She was then assimilated into the Greek pantheon and in early Greek writings between 800 and 479 BCE, Hekate was a benign figure, not yet associated with magic and witchery.

In Hesiod's *Theogony*, c. 700 BCE, Hekate was said to be the daughter of the Titans Perses and Asteria. Despite the Titans being overthrown by the Olympian gods, Zeus, their king, favoured Hekate greatly and she received her share of honour. A benign and helpful goddess, Hekate was frequently prayed to, with many asking for her favour.

The first seeds of Hekate's current identity are sown in Homer's *Hymn to Demeter*. Written in the late 7th or early

6th century BCE. In it the goddess is explicitly linked to the Underworld – according to the text, the 'tender-hearted' Hekate witnessed the abduction of Persephone and became the girl's attendant to escort her from the upper to the lower world, and back again. From this point, Hekate quickly became established as a liminal goddess: a guide during periods of transition, and by the Classical and Hellenistic periods, she became clearly associated with ghosts and magic. This Hekate strikes a terrifying figure indeed: haunting crossroads with her hounds and glowing torches, she is at one with the shadows, a chthonic goddess of the night. In the 1st century CE, Virgil uses 'Hekate's Grove' to describe the entrance to Hell, and the goddess also came to be associated with necromancy and sorcery, further cementing her reputation.

Hekate was originally portrayed as a single figure, but from the 5th century BCE was increasingly depicted as a triple goddess with each of her three faces looking in a different direction. This is a reflection of her connection to crossroads, and her strong association with boundaries or borders of many kinds, such as the thresholds between places, realms or events. This further strengthened her link with the dead, as restless spirits, often those who had died before their time or in a violent and bloody manner, were said to gather at crossroads. It was believed that such spirits – and Hekate herself who ruled over them – needed to be appeased, and so *deipna* – suppers of cakes, bread, garlic and cheese – were left as offerings at crossroads for the goddess in the hope that she would give protection in return.

In Euripides's play *Medea*, dating to the 5th century BCE, Hekate is shown clearly as a patron of vengeful magic and the Underworld, both furthering her connection with witches and bringing this reputation to a wider audience. Hekate is also invoked in curse tablets starting from this time, and examples include requests to bring an individual to ruin, or requesting that she, along with other deities, inflict someone with madness.

Witches are often said to possess the ability to transform others, and throughout ancient writings Hekate is linked with several instances of human-into-animal transformation. According to *On the Characteristics of Animals* by Aelian (from around the turn of the 2nd century BCE), Hekate, incensed by the sorceress Gale – well known for her inability to control her behaviour and her unnatural sexual appetites – turns her into a foul-smelling polecat.

Another human-to-polecat transformation linked to Hekate was that of Galinthias, who was transformed by the goddess Hera in punishment for her intervention during the birth of the demigod Herakles. Hera's husband Zeus had got the mortal Alkmene pregnant. Angry at her husband's infidelity, Hera instructed the *Moirai* – the Fates in Greek mythology – to withhold their customary help during her labour. Accordingly, the *Moirai* stood by the suffering woman's bedside with their arms folded, ignoring her increasing torment. Galinthias, Alkmene's friend or servant, was unable to stand the sight any longer, and tricked the Fates by saying that Alkmene had given birth to a boy – in their surprise, they unfolded their arms, thus allowing Alkmene to give birth at last. For her mercy, Galinthias paid a terrible price: Hera turned her into a polecat. In this story, Hekate was the saviour of the piece, as she was said to have taken pity on poor Galinthias in her new form and adopted her as a servant.

Hekate was also associated with dogs or hounds, and she is sometimes depicted with either a single dog or a whole pack. One tale suggests that her canine companion was in fact the Trojan Queen Hekabe or Hecuba. After the fall of Troy, the distraught queen leapt into the sea, seeking to end her life; there

Hekate transformed her into dog form, and she remained with the goddess from then on.

In modern Wicca today, Hekate is said to represent the Great Goddess in her Crone form. She is a popular deity, invoked for guidance and protection, in particular where transitions are concerned. Hekate is still associated with witchcraft, the moon, crossroads and the Underworld, and rituals are performed in her name, in particular on the nights of the new moon and the Gaelic seasonal festival of Samhain.

Hekate hasn't just been a source of inspiration in the art world, but also makes appearances across theatre, television and literature. One of her earliest cameos is in one of Shakespeare's most famous plays: *Macbeth*. There she is portrayed as the merciless leader of the witches. Appearing in two scenes, she first rebukes the three witches for sharing prophecies with Macbeth without her say so, and, later, she returns to commend them on the spells they have cast. It is thought that Hekate may not have been an original character in the play, but that her scenes were added during the editing of the First Folio, potentially by the English playwright Thomas Middleton.

In more recent times, Hekate has continued to fascinate, with portrayals of the goddess varying in their degree of creative license. Among others, she is referenced in three episodes of *Buffy the Vampire Slayer*, and in the 1998 film *Practical Magic* starring Nicole Kidman and Sandra Bullock, and is clearly considered a powerful witch in both. In the TV show *Charmed*, she is portrayed as Queen of the Underworld, a figure that is more demon than goddess. In literature, Hekate appears several times throughout Rick Riordan's *Percy Jackson* series, in which the background assigned to the goddess is largely faithful to her original roots.

Double, Double, Toil and Trouble:
The Witches of *Macbeth*

Fair is foul, and foul is fair
Hover through the fog and filthy air . . .

The image of Macbeth meeting the three witches who foretell his future greatness and equally spectacular downfall is deeply ingrained in the popular consciousness. Who exactly were these mysterious beings, and what were their origins?

Macbeth was first performed in or around 1606, at a time when witches were a hot topic throughout Europe. In *Holinshed's Chronicles*, the original source material used by Shakespeare that was published around 30 years earlier, the witches are described as 'three women in strange and wild apparel, resembling creatures of elder world'. Likewise in *Macbeth*, in appearance the characters are very witch-like indeed: withered and wrinkled, with chapped fingers, and thin, 'skinny' lips; they are clearly identifiable to both contemporaries and modern audiences as the well-known hag-like witch figure. The actions they discuss would have also

been clearly recognizable to contemporary audiences as those of witches: one says she has been killing swine, while another admits to plaguing the sailor husband of a woman who denied her, sending storms and sickness to him in revenge. These were common accusations against witches throughout the period and beyond.

The iconic cauldron scene further supports the identification of the three sisters as witches. Among the myriad gruesome ingredients mentioned is 'finger of birth-strangled babe', alluding to the fact that witches were said to use the bodies of unbaptized children in their wicked concoctions. 'Root of hemlock digg'd i' the dark' and 'slips of yew' were also closely associated with witchcraft, as were the many other ingredients listed such as toads and frogs. It appears therefore that the three are witches, through and through.

The matter may not, however, be so clear-cut. Although listed as witches, in the text of the First Folio edition of 1623 the women are referred to as 'weyward' or 'weyard' sisters, a fact that has sparked debate regarding the exact identity of Macbeth's 'witches'. The first explanation is the simplest: wayward, meaning obstinate, unruly and stubborn, simply describes the witch-like personalities of the three. Some, however, highlight that 'weyard' actually pertains to 'wyrd', implying a somewhat different origin. Wyrd was an Anglo-Saxon and Scandinavian term meaning fateful or having to do with fate and, in Old Norse, one of the Norns – or Fates, of whom there were also three – is often named Wyrd. It is suggested therefore that the three sisters were in fact actually goddesses or beings of fate and destiny; the prophetic role they take on in the play likewise hinting at this dual identity. Holinshed also refers to the three women as 'weird', stating that 'the common opinion was that these women were either the Weird Sisters... the goddesses of destiny, or else some nymphs or fairies endued with knowledge of prophecy by their necromantical science,' and Shakespeare's witches likewise retain some of this function, performing several acts of prophecy throughout the play.

Whether witch or fate or something in between, the 'Weird Sisters' have long exerted a powerful hold over our imaginations, and have been depicted in a variety of ways in both works of art and fiction. There have been at least 40 film adaptations of the play, and the witches have been adapted to various different cultures, such as their portrayal as voodoo priestesses in the 1948 film by Orson Welles. The witches were also utilized for political satire: in 1791 James Gillray parodied the famous painting of the witches by Henry Fuseli in a piece called *Weird Sisters; Ministers of Darkness; Minions of the Moon*, in which he inserted the then home secretary, prime minister and lord chancellor in place of the witches.

Macbeth's witches also feature in one of the best-known superstitions of the theatre. According to popular belief, the play itself is cursed, and it all stems back to these characters. As legend has it, the Witches' incantations included by Shakespeare were actually real spells and this so angered a local coven that real witches cursed the play. As a result, the first actor cast as Lady Macbeth is said to have died before opening night, forcing Shakespeare to play the part himself. Thus began a long line of tragedies and mishaps ascribed to the power of the curse: from Laurence Olivier narrowly escaping death when a stage weight of over 11kg (25lb) nearly landed on him, to the 1849 Astor Place Riot in New York between two rival companies over the correct interpretation of *Macbeth*, which resulted in the death of at least 22 people.

From Dame Gothel to Hansel and Gretel:
Witches in Folk and Fairy Tales

Fairy tales and folk tales are, for many of us, our first introduction to the idea of witches. Whether being read 'Hansel and Gretel' as a bedtime story, or watching a production of *The Snow Queen* on stage, witches and witch-like characters are introduced into our subconscious from our earliest days. Details may vary from place to place, from culture to culture, but the main characteristics of the witch within these tales are remarkably consistent and provide a fascinating insight into our deepest, darkest fears and imaginings.

One thing that is immediately clear is that witches in such tales are nearly always women. This is unsurprising, and reflects the fact that historically, in many areas, it was mainly women who were accused of witchcraft. Although a significant number of men were in fact also named as witches, in the fictional realm male characters that practise harmful magic are instead usually called wizards or sorcerers, and are viewed differently as a consequence by both readers and other characters within the story.

Although fairy and folk tales have diverse plots and messages, it is possible to loosely identify several broad 'types' when it comes to the witch. The most common witch type is that of the evil, malevolent witch, using her powers for nefarious purposes. Inherently bad, the actions of this witch are selfishly motivated, and she has little or no redeeming features. In such tales, the outward appearance of the witch usually matches their ugly inner selves: old and haggard, with a hooked nose and dressed in rags, they are, quite simply, the stereotypical fairy-tale witch that we have come to expect.

One well-known example is the witch from 'Hansel and Gretel', as recorded in *Kinder und Hausmärchen* or *Grimms' Fairy Tales*, first published in 1812. Living in the middle of the forest in her house made of bread, with cake for a roof and clear sugar windows, she lures the unsuspecting children into her lair with the promise of help, but with the plan to fatten them up and eat them. The idea of the cannibal-witch was a prevalent popular belief, and this very real fear is often reflected in such tales, further illustrating the evil nature of the witch.

Deceit is another common trait. In the Romanian tale, 'The Morning Star and the Evening Star', the young Siminok encounters a wicked witch in the woods while looking for his lost brother. She promises him aid but, unsurprisingly to the reader, goes back on her word, threatening – in another case of the cannibal-witch trope – to eat him. However, the young man is well prepared for her treachery, and the witch is torn apart by his dogs in a satisfying triumph of good over evil.

There are countless other examples of the stereotypical evil witch, and in these tales the witch frequently represents the epitome of all evil, in stark contrast to the pure and good hero or heroine. These witches most often come to a bad end, which is considered a necessary and just punishment for their wicked ways.

Another familiar trait of the fairy-tale witch is that of shape-shifting. While generally portrayed as old and ugly, in 'Hansel and Gretel' the witch is able to alter her appearance to be more pleasant in order to trick her young victims. In the Russian fairy tale 'The White Duck', the king tells his new wife not to leave her quarters while he is away on a journey. The queen is tempted outside, however, by a wicked witch who transforms her into a duck, while changing her own appearance into that of the queen so that she can take her place.

There are also many instances of a witch changing the form of another character. Márya Tsarévna's witch-like stepmother in 'The Dun Cow' employs transformative magic to change the girl into a goose so that her own daughter can marry the handsome prince. Márya is transformed in turn into a frog, a lizard, various insects, and finally a spindle before, thanks to the determination of the prince, she regains her human form. In 'The Fair Angiola', an Italian tale by Thomas Frederick Crane, the witch transforms Angiola's face into that of a dog. Unusually, at the end of the story the witch is merciful and removes the enchantment. In 'The Twelve Wild Ducks' from Norway, a wicked witch transforms the 12 sons of the queen into wild ducks. They are ultimately saved by their devoted sister, who remains silent for seven years while sewing 12 shirts from nettle leaves, thus freeing them from the enchantment and the witch's power. This idea is the theme of several other tales that follow a broadly similar storyline, including Hans Christian Andersen's popular 'The Wild Swans'.

Self-serving and duplicitous by nature, a witch is often seen to make a bargain with the protagonist or another character. At these times, the witch preys on an individual's weakness or need, granting help in return for a terrible price. In the Danish tale 'The White Dove', two princes promise their unborn younger sibling to a witch in return for saving their lives at sea, a bargain made in the face of great peril that they would live to regret once the immediate danger was past.

Fairy-tale witches are often shunned by their local community and therefore are often found living in remote locations such as in caves or forests, further reinforcing the image of the witch as 'other' and outside of normal, civilized society. Perhaps most famously, Baba Yaga, the popular witch featured in many Slavic tales, lives deep in the forest in her chicken-legged hut. In the German 'Jorinde and Joringel', the titular characters discover a witch's castle after venturing through a mysterious forest. This isolated location is a useful plot device, and often the protagonist must find the witch in order to complete their quest or journey; or sometimes, it is upon discovering a witch in her out-of-the-way abode that a quest is issued.

When portrayed as evil, with few or no redeeming features, the witch often meets a bad end. In some versions of 'The Three Golden Hairs', the witch's power is broken when the protagonist manages to pluck the three golden hairs that are the seat of all her power. The witch then vanishes and the child she has stolen is rescued, a demonstrable triumph of good over evil. In 'The Witch in the Stone Boat' from Iceland, a village is under the power of an evil witch. Erik, the brave protagonist – armed with a charm from a 'wise old woman' in his village – is victorious and the witch is defeated. Some conclusions are particularly apt: in 'Hansel and Gretel' the witch meets her end in the very oven where she had planned to cook the children, while in 'The Golden Bird' the witch dies when her own tree falls on her.

On closer examination, however, in some tales there are definite grey areas where the witch is concerned. For example, there are instances where a witch is – at least initially – the wronged party. In 'Rapunzel', Rapunzel's father steals from the sorceress, Dame Gothel. Readers are told that although she is initially angry, after hearing his pleas regarding the cravings of his pregnant wife, the witch softens slightly and, rather than dealing out a violent punishment, makes a bargain to take the child instead, promising to be a good mother to her. Likewise, in 'The Fair Angiola', seven women creep into the witch's garden to steal the jujubes that grow there, effectively carrying out a crime. In the English tale 'The Old Witch' as told by Joseph Jacobs, two girls who are unable to get jobs elsewhere go in turn to work for a witch. The witch tells the girls not to look up the chimney, but, of course, temptation wins out: both look, and when they do, bags of money fall down into the fireplace. Both girls take the money and, understandably, the angry witch follows to get her fortune back. The girl who has worked hard and has treated others well manages to escape with the help of those she has assisted throughout the course of the story. The selfish girl, on the other hand, receives no help and the witch beats her and takes back her money. Although the first girl has stolen just as the lazy girl has, her actions are deemed acceptable simply because she is 'good', while the witch is portrayed as inherently bad.

Revealingly, the witch is still ultimately considered the villain, regardless of how she has been treated. This highlights the contradiction of the witch: while powerful and greatly feared, she is at the same time powerless against her reputation and the label that has been foisted upon her. A witch, by dint of being a witch, is wicked, and therefore all of her actions and words reinforce and prove this, leaving, in most cases, no chance of redemption.

It is interesting to note that positive figures who use their magical powers for good are often not explicitly referred to as witches. Although they have the same powers as the evil witch, they lack the destructive element possessed by their less popular counterparts, and therefore are often referred to as the more positive 'wise women' or 'good fairies'. A well-known witch-like figure that works for good is the Fairy Godmother from the story of 'Cinderella'. Referred to only as 'the fairy' in the earliest version of this tale, in future retellings she has fully developed into the fairy godmother figure, human in form with magical powers. Through her intervention, Cinderella manages to go to the ball and eventually marry the prince, her life ultimately improved and transformed.

Some tales offer the witch a second chance. In 'The Witch of the Ardennes' from Belgium, the witch turns out to be misunderstood rather than evil. Rumoured to have sinister powers, and living deep in the woods, local legend warns of the wicked spells she casts on any who go too near. The protagonist of the tale decides to venture into the woods to discover the truth, however, and finds, rather than a terrifying figure, a kindly old healer. It transpires that she used to help people with her herbs and spells, but through fear, jealousy and misunderstanding, people had turned against her and she had fled the village. When this information is relayed to the villagers, the situation is quickly resolved: people readjust their views and the witch is welcomed back into the community and respected once more. This highlights the very fine line between good and bad magic, and how easily a reputation could switch from one to the other.

The Witch with the Chicken-Legged Hut:
Baba Yaga

One of the most iconic and well-known fairy-tale witches is the Slavic Baba Yaga. Living in the deepest of forests in her hut – with its chicken-leg stilts and a fence of skull-topped human bones – Baba Yaga is, on the surface, the epitome of the evil fairy-tale witch. Ancient and ugly, with a stooping figure and long hooked nose, the intimidating image is completed with sharp iron teeth, making her a figure that strikes fear into even the bravest of hearts.

Sometimes Baba Yaga is said to fly on a broom, but her preferred mode of transport is a large mortar, and she can be seen flying in it just above the ground, steering with her equally large pestle. In some tales, she is portrayed as a cannibal witch, and the villain of many a story has sent the hero or heroine to find Baba Yaga in the secret hope that they will be eaten.

Beneath the surface, however, Baba Yaga is a complex character rather than a one-dimensional stereotype. Clever and resourceful, she also recognizes and appreciates these same qualities in others. In 'Vasilisa the Beautiful', a young woman is sent to fetch fire from Baba Yaga's hut by her jealous stepmother. When she completes the difficult tasks set for her, Baba Yaga is greatly impressed and gives the girl the fire she seeks. In 'Ivan

Tsarevich, the Firebird, and the Grey Wolf', Ivan finds himself needing guidance from Baba Yaga on how to find the Firebird. Again, she sets tasks for the protagonist, testing him to see if he is worthy of her help. It is clear from many stories involving Baba Yaga that this wise witch can influence the outcome of a quest by giving or refusing her aid, highlighting the great power she holds both in magical terms and also in her ability to impact the story as a whole.

The earliest written mention of Baba Yaga is believed to be from the 1755 *Russian Grammar* by Mikhail V. Lomonosov, where she is named along with a list of other Slavic deities and beings. There are many tales of her from Russia, where she is a central and popular figure in folklore, and she is also present in stories from Ukraine, Poland, the Czech Republic and Slovakia. Through translation and, more recently, the impact of the internet, tales of Baba Yaga have spread across the globe, and today interest in this popular and intriguing character remains undiminished. *Into the Forest*, an anthology of short stories published in 2022 interpreting and re-imagining Baba Yaga across history, perfectly highlights the timeless lure of one of fairy tale's greatest witches.

Milk Magic:
Butter Stealing and Milk Thieves

For much of human history, dairy farming and milk production, and by extension the various commodities connected to them, have been of crucial importance to rural economies throughout Europe. When the health of the milk yield could be the difference between survival and death, it was vital to protect every step of the process, from the cows chewing cud in the fields to the milk churn in the dairy.

When cows suddenly produced less milk than they used to, or butter refused to churn, what – or who – was to blame? Witches, both in legend and in reality, were often a convenient scapegoat for such disasters, with the idea that a witch could directly interfere with milk production lingering in several areas of Europe well into the 20th century.

According to popular belief, a witch could steal milk in a variety of ways. One method was to transform into animal form – most commonly that of a hare – in order to suckle the milk directly from cows and sheep. This idea has a long history: for example, the 12th-century *Topographia Hiberniae* by Giraldus Cambrensis (Gerald of Wales) records the popular belief in

Ireland that witches turned themselves into hares to steal milk from the herds, and it was likewise documented elsewhere.

To make matters worse, the witch didn't always need to be present in order to carry out such thefts: there were several methods whereby the witch could accomplish her aim from a safe distance. In Germany, it was believed that a witch could steal milk by sticking an axe or knife into a doorpost. In New England, there was the similar idea of tying a rag to an axe handle or fence post. Similarly, in Norway, Germany and Austria, it was said that the witch could draw milk using a knife or her garter.

Another popular method of milk stealing was through the gathering of dew. It was believed that when a witch gathered dew it represented the milk from the herd, and therefore collecting it meant that the witch had likewise collected the milk, transferring it to her own cows. Dew could be obtained in several ways, such as drawing a rope – generally made from hair – over the grass, while reciting words such as, 'Come all to me.'

In Transylvania, in modern-day Romania, belief in dew-collecting witches was also common, and they were said to be particularly prolific on important agricultural festivals and holidays. A piece of cloth or a strainer was pulled over the grass to collect the dew, while words such as the following were recited: 'As in this manner the dew is picked from the grass, likewise the milk yield is collected from all the cows bringing it only to my cows.' The dew would then be fed to the witch's cows and the transfer would be complete. Similarly, in Zagreb in the 17th and 18th centuries, witches were said to collect dew with their left hand from the crossroads early in the morning during the week of the new moon for this purpose.

Milk theft by witches was likewise central to Polish witchcraft belief. In 1674, Dorotea Pilecka became implicated in accusations of witchcraft when another woman, Krystyna

Gajowa Danielecka, named her as a witch. Washing cattle in herbs, collecting manure, soil and grass from the hoofprints of people's cattle, gathering herbs in the local cemetery and attending calvings in order to take the afterbirth were among the charges made against Dorotea, all of which were believed to have the purpose of increasing the milk production of her own cows at the expense of others. Although she didn't confess, even under torture, Dorotea was found guilty and executed by beheading.

However, people also believed there were ways to protect against milk-stealing witches. Prevention was better than cure, and flowers could be tied to the tails or horns of cows, or to the milk churn itself, in order to ward off witches. Lightly charring a hair on the head of each animal or striking them with a berry switch were other methods of protection, recorded towards the end of the 19th century in County Wexford, Ireland.

If the milk had already been stolen and cows were visibly producing less milk, it was not too late to rectify the situation. Heating herbs along with some milk and then adding new pins or needles would make the witch writhe in agony. She would then come running in an attempt to stop the process and relieve her pain. If the identity of the witch was known or suspected, then taking fire from the individual's house could counteract her actions, as could burning the thatch from the roof above the door of the milk-stealer's house.

In Vlasenica, Bosnia, it was believed that if a moth flew into a house at night it was a witch coming to take milk from the cows. To foil the theft, it was essential to catch the moth, sprinkle it with salt, and eject it from the house with the words: 'Go off, and come tomorrow to get some salt.' If the next day a woman came to borrow salt, then she was the milk thief.

In Ireland, milk stealing was believed to be particularly prevalent on May Day (1st May). Flowers were strewn across the window ledges and thresholds on May Eve in preparation, with primroses and marigolds being popular choices. If a hare was seen in the cattle on that day, it was believed to be a witch and should therefore be killed as it had come to steal milk. Likewise in Denmark, southwestern Sweden and southern Norway, as well as the British Isles and other parts of Europe, there was a belief that witches turned into hares in order to carry out mischief, with stealing milk one of the main crimes of choice.

Another popular idea in Ireland was that it was a bad idea to give anything away or to let anything leave the house on May Day, as it was believed that this could then be used against the household in the form of milk stealing. There was great suspicion, therefore, of anyone who visited a house after sunset on May Day Eve and on May Day itself, especially if they were an old, poor widow.

In Transylvania, milk witches were said to be most active on St John's Day (24 June), St Andrew's Day (30 November) and, most of all, on St George's Day (23 April). This belief was persistent throughout villages in Romania until at least the end of the 19th century: it was believed that a milk witch took water from the river that sheep crossed and then gave it to her own sheep to increase their milk at the expense of others. In parts of Serbia, it was believed that on St George's Day local witches rode naked round the village on weaving beams, which would transfer milk to their own pails for the year ahead.

Milk Hares and Troll Cats

In the quest to steal milk, a witch had another option available: creating a creature that would do the work for her. In areas of northern Europe this idea was particularly popular, and it was even said to be possible for a witch to have more than one milk thief to do her bidding.

Such a creature could take various forms and had different names from place to place. In Norway and Sweden, it was generally known as a *bjara* (meaning carrier) or troll cat. Sometimes a troll cat took the form of an actual cat but, despite its name, a more common appearance was that of a grey ball.

A troll cat was commonly made from a combination of wood shavings, human nails and hair. In Sweden, c.1900, one old woman was said to have used knitting needles and rags to make her milk theives, while wooden pegs and a stocking leg was another popular combination.

In southwest Sweden and in a couple of examples from Norway, the creature was known as the *mjölkhare* or milkhare, constructed from heddles (part of a loom), bits of wood, or bits of besoms and scrubbing brooms. The creation of such a creature was no idle undertaking, and the witch was said to have sold her soul in order to give the troll cat life.

One ingredient in particular was vital: a drop of the witch's blood to animate the creature. According to popular belief, the witch would drip blood onto the bundle, while reciting a spell such as: 'I give you blood, Satan gives you power. You shall run for me on earth, I shall burn for you in Hell. You shall travel through forests and fields, gathering milk and cream.'

The witch would then send the creature out to steal milk for her. In the form of a grey or brown ball of yarn, the troll cat rolled its way from one cow to the next, sucking milk from each in turn. When full, it would roll itself homewards to where the witch waited, ready to receive the milk it spat out into her pails.

When the troll cat took the form of an actual cat, it was believed that if such a creature was injured it would cause direct harm to the witch who owned it. However, if in ball form, then the witch felt nothing, and only the troll cat was destroyed. When the witch died, it was essential for the troll cat to go with her to the grave: if it did not, then the witch would not rest and would return to claim it. Belief in troll cats and their association with witches was at times so strong that actual cats were attacked in the belief that they were milk stealers.

One possible explanation for belief in troll cats is *aegagropila* – undigested matter found in cow faeces. When dry, this substance blows across the ground and may appear like a living creature, thus giving rise to ideas of the milk-stealing troll cat. Similarly, there was a widespread belief that it was possible to inflict harm on the witch that had created the creature by burning troll-cat vomit, and that doing so would bring great pain. Well known for overindulgence, the troll cat would often drink more milk than it had room for, leaking excess milk known variously as grey-paw butter, troll-cat butter, troll-cat vomit or *Tusse-dung*. This 'evidence' of the troll cat was often found the morning after it had been out causing mischief: in reality, this 'vomit' was really algae, insect secretions or a type of fungus.

In Sweden, there are some legends where the making of the troll cat goes horribly wrong or someone who has observed a witch making one tries to replicate the process. The observer often gets more than they bargained for, when, instead of producing milk, their creature produces excrement instead!

In Iceland, tales of similar milk-stealing creatures have existed since the 17th century, where they were generally referred to as *tilberi* or carriers. In southern Iceland the creature is known as a *snakkur*, meaning spindle. To create a carrier, the witch would take a rib from a recent grave early in the morning on Whitsuntide. This would then be wrapped in some stolen grey wool before being concealed in the witch's bosom. When attending church, instead of swallowing the communion wine, the witch would spit it onto the bundle hidden in her chest, until it eventually came alive.

Once sent out by the witch, the creature would elongate itself and stretch over the cow to reach the teats from both sides. It was generally believed to have a mouth on each end and to suck in tandem for increased efficiency, but some believed it to have only one mouth, moving systematically from one side of the cow to the other.

Full of milk, the carrier grew to be like an 'inflated oblong balloon'. It would then return home to its 'mother' with the words: 'Churn lid off, Mother!' or 'Full belly, Mother!' Hearing this, the witch would remove the lid from the churn and the tilberi would vomit the milk into it. In reward, the witch then fed the creature with blood from her inner thigh – over time this was said to cause a wart-like growth that could be used as proof that she was a witch.

Like the troll cat, tilberi were prone to overfeeding at times: if they took in more than their stomachs could hold, they would vomit onto the ground – the lichen *Cetraria islandica* or Iceland moss was often said to be tilberi vomit or spew.

Belief in the tilberi was enduring and well into the 19th century it was still common practice to make a protective cross on a cow – going under the animal's udders and over the rump – before laying a psalter against its spine. Tilberi were often blamed for a common disease that afflicted the udders of both cows and ewes, as it was said that the affected animals had been sucked by these creatures. It was also said to be easy to identify butter made from milk stolen by the tilberi: if the sign of the cross was made over the butter or if it was marked with a cross, it would curdle and clot, before reducing down to little flakes or froth.

It was believed that if the tilberi felt threatened, like any child, it would run to its mother and hide under her skirts. Then, if the witch's petticoats were quickly tied underneath it, the creature could be trapped and then either drowned or burned. There were also certain dangers in creating a tilberi – if the witch that made it also had her own human child, it was possible for the creature to try to feed from her breasts and suck her to death.

I Shall Go Into A Hare:
The Hare and the Witch

Witches were often said to be able to transform into an animal at will. One of the animals a witch was most commonly said to change into was a hare, and this concept is frequently found in fairy tales and legends across many areas of Europe and beyond.

A popular framework for such a story involves a hare that is noted for being faster than all the rest, evading capture no matter how fast the hounds, or how true the farmer's shot. Day after day, the hare escapes, with its pursuers growing more and more frustrated. Success seems impossible, until someone suggests the use of a silver bullet: this, of course, leads to the injuring of the animal, as silver is well known to be effective against all manner of supernatural foes.

Sometimes the hare escapes, only for it to be revealed that a local old woman – very often one suspected of being a witch – has suffered grievous injuries, which just so happen to be in the very same location as the hare's, thus revealing that hare and witch are one and the same.

In a German tale, 'The Girl Who Transformed Herself into a Hare', a young girl inherits a witch's leather thong from her grandmother. Able to transform herself into a hare by tying

the thong around herself, she does so frequently, delighting in tormenting a local forester when in her hare form: even though the man shoots at her many times, his bullets always slide off, completely harmless. Finally realizing that this is no natural hare, the forester loads his gun with an iron coffin nail instead: he hits the hare and the injured creature immediately turns into the girl, her foot bloody and her identity revealed. In another story from Germany, 'Witch as Hare', a hare again taunts a hunter who is unable to catch it. This time consecrated powder brings success, and the injured hare transforms into a woman. As in many tales of this type, the wound proves fatal, providing a handy cautionary moral regarding the pitfalls of being corrupted by witchcraft.

In the Danish 'A Witch in Hare-Skin', a hare has been stealing cabbages from the almshouse garden during a bad winter when food was scarce for all. A hunter tries to shoot it but, despite firing multiple shots at the hare, the animal remains unscathed. His father, a skilled marksman, bends a silver shilling with a cross on it and loads it into his gun; the hare is hit, and there, in its place, is an old woman from the town. The shilling sticks firmly in her forehead, and the mark it leaves means that she will not be able to transform ever again.

Such tales of transforming witch-hares were particularly popular in the British Isles. In 'The Shot Hare' from Wales, Beti Ifan, an old woman known to be a witch, transforms herself into a hare to torment a local poacher who has teased her. Despite being a good shot, the poacher never manages to hit the hare, so he consults with a cunning man who tells him to take a small branch of mountain ash and a sprig of vervain and put them under the gun stock. The man is also given a piece of paper containing words that he is to recite when he sees the creature. Then, he is told, he will see it in its true form, but he must shoot at the hare's legs, even though he sees her as the woman she is. The man follows these instructions to the letter, and after shooting at the hare it runs towards Beti's cottage, where he finds the woman bleeding and in great pain. After this, the man is no longer bothered by the hare again.

The idea of the witch's ability to transform into a hare wasn't just confined to stories: sometimes those accused of witchcraft likewise admitted to such transformations. Famed Scottish witch Isobel Gowdie confessed that she had, on more than one occasion, transformed into a hare with the words: 'I shall go into a hare, with sorrow and such and meickle [great] care; and I shall go in the Devil's name, ay while I come home again.' She recounted also how she had transformed herself back in the nick of time when being chased by dogs with the words: 'Hare, hare, God send thee care! I am in a hare's likeness now; but I shall be woman even now – hare, hare, God send thee care!'

Hares generally had a bad press, a reputation that stretches back to ancient times. In the Book of Deuteronomy in the Bible, the animal is named as unclean and therefore not fit to eat, a belief that was also present in England around 50 BCE, and that is perhaps linked to their use for divinatory purposes. In 19th-century Kerry, Ireland, it was said that people in the countryside didn't eat hares because they contained the souls of their grandmothers. The supposed link between witches and hares meant they were viewed with added suspicion, as any hare could be a witch in disguise. Meeting a hare or one crossing your path was considered to be bad luck in many areas, though carrying the right foot from a dead hare was actually said to provide protection from witchcraft.

From Alewives to the Wicked Witch of the West:
Why Do Witches Wear Pointed Hats?

Ask anyone in the United Kingdom or the USA to identify an accessory most associated with a witch's appearance and the chances are that 'pointed hat' will be top of the list. Our story books, popular art and movies are filled with cone-shaped-hat-wearing witches – not least of all the iconic depiction of the stereotypical evil witch played by Margaret Hamilton in *The Wizard of Oz* – and it is the easy go-to for a costume at Halloween. There is no denying that the connection between witches and pointed hats has become deeply entrenched in our collective psyches. But where did this association first come from?

The truth of the matter is that ultimately no one really knows for certain when or how the link between witches and the now iconic hat started. As is the case with many things, it is highly likely that there was no one, single, point of origin, and that the association we have today comes from a blend of different starting points and ideas.

One often-cited origin theory is that of the Jewish Hat or Judenhat. Appearances varied, but a common design was a hat with a stiff, circular brim, curving round to a tapered and often pointed top, that was originally worn by choice but later enforced upon Jewish men in some areas of Europe in the 13th century. Jews were ostracized as a dangerous and heretical group, and the theory goes that the deliberate linking of them to witches by those in authority via such a readily identifiable accessory meant that witches would likewise be feared and persecuted. There is a flaw in this theory, however, as Jews in England were not required to wear such a hat and instead wore a 'distinguishing mark' made of yellow felt on their clothing. As a hat was not associated with English Jews, it was unlikely therefore that such a connection would be made between their hats and witches.

Another theory linking witch hats with persecuted groups involves the Quakers. This 17th-century religious sect were treated with great suspicion, and their beliefs, in particular concerning conferring equality to women within the sect, were seen as outlandish and dangerous by many. In a variety of prints from the time, Quaker women can be seen wearing a high-crowned hat, similar to that which we now identify with witches, and it has been suggested that witches were portrayed wearing the same headgear as a handy method of increasing the persecution of both groups.

Then there is the popular idea of alewives. According to this argument, alewives in the Middle Ages wore pointed hats to stand out to customers through the crowded market place. Their brewing and concocting of 'potions' with herbs etc. was not a far cry from the supposed sorcery of witches, and the hat and witch thus became conflated. Some also believe that, in an underhand exploitation of gender politics, male ale-makers sowed the seeds to discredit their female counterparts by linking them and their headwear to witches in order to take control of the market.

The closest answer to the truth, however, might be much simpler. In the 17th century, there developed a fashion for women wearing high-crowned hats, and there are many portraits of women wearing these hats throughout the period. It is possible therefore that this style of hat became associated with witches due simply to the fact that women often wore hats of a pointed style – and as women were mainly those targeted as witches, the two became associated.

What is certain is that the image of the witch with a pointed hat was established in woodcuts from at least the 18th century onwards, and it was a familiar enough concept by that time that it required no explanation to audiences. Such imagery served to further cement the idea that such a hat was a standard identifying feature of a witch, creating a snowball effect down through the ages. The idea was so completely ingrained that by the 1970s, when prehistoric skeletons were discovered in the Tarim Basin in Eastern Central Asia with the remains of tall, pointed, fabric-like hats, they became popularly known as the 'Witches of Subeshi', despite having no known connection to witchcraft or magic.

Whatever the origin, one thing is abundantly clear: the image of the witch wearing a pointed hat is here to stay.

Perchta the Belly Slitter and other Midwinter Witches

Although nowadays, once Halloween is past, ghosts and spirits are replaced with bauble-covered Christmas trees and gaily wrapped presents, this has not always been the case. The midwinter period has long been associated with witches, and across Europe there are several terrifying witch-like figures closely tied to the winter festivities.

Perchta

Perchta, or Frau Perchta, is a figure from Germanic folklore, hugely popular across the alpine regions of Austria, Germany and Switzerland. According to legend, this winter witch is most active during the 12 days of Christmas – between 25 December and 6 January – when she goes visiting from house to house. For those who have behaved all year round there is nothing to fear, and Perchta will leave

a silver coin – *Perchtenlauben* – in their shoe. Those who have behaved badly, however, beware: Perchta will slit their stomachs open and pull out their innards, before stuffing the empty space with straw.

Perchta's original purpose was as punisher of those who broke cultural taboos. From the mid-16th century she was closely linked with spinning, and she was a keen enforcer of rules surrounding this occupation, punishing those who spun at night or on certain feasts or holidays when it was forbidden.

In appearance, Perchta is – in keeping with her actions – terrifying. She is generally said to be a ragged crone or hag, with an iron, beak-like nose, unkempt clothes and hair, and the long, sharp knife she uses for her bloody task concealed in her skirts. In some accounts Perchta has another readily identifiable feature: one foot is said to be much larger than the other.

It has recently been suggested that Perchta could have originated as a personification of Epiphany, the Christian festival that falls on 6 January, itself. The name Perchta – or Percht or Berchte as she is sometimes called – seems to have first been mentioned in the 13th century, and by the following century she was established as being linked to the 12 days of Christmas. She was well known as a spirit to whom people left offerings at that time: a later source lists cheese, bread, milk, eggs, wine and water as suitable gifts.

Over time, Perchta's spinning-specific role shifted until she became a general punisher of the lazy. In some areas of Austria between Salzburg and Styria, Perchta was said to slit the stomachs of generally indolent people and fill them with splinters of glass, chaff, and dust and rubbish from the floor. As well as her signature belly-slitting, other punishments were sometimes attributed to Perchta; at Schottwien, to the southwest of Vienna, Perchta was said to scrape the tongues of lying children with glass.

Another belief connected to Perchta found in Styria and elsewhere was that having a firm, full belly at Epiphany could mean that Perchta's knife would slide straight off if she tried to slit a person open. On the other hand, if an individual's belly was not full enough, Perchta would successfully disembowel them and stuff the empty cavity with rags. Generally a time of abundance and feasting, it was believed that eating heartily on 6 January would ensure there was plenty of food for the year ahead. To not do so would mean the opposite, a time of want and lack. The message was clear: eat well during Epiphany!

Perchta can also be understood as part of a developing tradition during the 9th century of a mysterious spectral female figure leading a procession of spirits and other females through the night. Linked with ideas of the Wild Hunt, Perchta is said to fly through the skies with her followers, the *Perchten*, and sometimes accompanied by the souls of unbaptized children.

Today, particularly in southern Germany and Austria, Perchta is used as a cautionary tale for children, and a handy incentive for good behaviour.

Frau Holle

Mother Holle or Frau Holle is another witch-like figure associated with the midwinter period. Some equate her with Perchta, and there are indeed several similarities between the two.

Like Perchta, Holle is associated with spinning. In Bohemia, Frau Holle carried a bunch of stinging nettles with which she would beat lazy spinners, and she punished those spinning at the prohibited time of St Thomas' Night – 21 December. There is also a popular theory that, like Perchta, Frau Holle was an ancient Germanic goddess. Some equate Holle with

Holda, goddess of the women's domain of the household, and in particular spinning and weaving.

Between Christmas and Twelfth Night, Holda was said to ride in her wagon across the fields, blessing them with fertility for the year ahead. Again like Perchta, she was sometimes also said to lead a sinister host composed of witches, the dead and the souls of unbaptized infants. It is possible that 'Holda' was not initially meant to represent an individual person or character at all. It has been suggested that in fact Holda originally referred to the night rides themselves and, over time, came to be taken as the name of the one who led them.

Holle is also said to bring the snow of the season with her, created by tossing up her eiderdown when she made the bed. In the Grimms' tale 'Frau Holle', a girl, mistreated by her stepmother, drops her spindle in the well while spinning one day. Terrified of what punishment awaits her, she leaps in to get it. Instead of landing at the bottom of the well, the girl finds herself in a magical land where there is plenty, with bread and apples and everything she could want. She comes across an old woman who takes her in; the woman introduces herself as Frau Holle, and says that if the girl will do her housework, then she will be fed and housed in return. The girl has one main task to do – shake out Frau Holle's bed so that the feathers fly and make snow in the human world. The girl works hard and, when she finally asks to go home, Frau Holle takes her back to her stepmother and rewards her with gold for her hard work. Wanting the same for her own daughter, the stepmother instructs her to do the same as her stepsister. But the girl is lazy and unpleasant, and Frau Holle is unimpressed: *her* reward is to be covered in pitch, highlighting the message that Frau Holle rewards the industrious and kind-hearted and punishes the idle and mean-spirited.

In modern folklore, Holle is particularly popular in Thuringia and Hesse in Germany, and is also found in Franconia and southern Saxony. Today she is not known for malevolent behaviour, but is a kind, positive force.

La Befana

Here comes, here comes the Befana, she comes from the mountains in the deep of the night. Look how tired she is! All wrapped up in snow and frost and the north wind! Here comes, here comes the Befana!

Italy's La Befana is an example of a benevolent witch-like figure associated with winter. She has deep roots in Italy's Christmas and Epiphany traditions and is hugely popular throughout the country, in particular in southern and central Italy, as well as in places throughout the world with large Italian communities.

Although not explicitly referred to as a witch, La Befana is often depicted as old and haggard in appearance, flying through the air on her broomstick: she enters houses down the chimney, which is why her black shawl is always covered in soot. Despite her questionable appearance, La Befana is said to have a smile on her face, and she brings with her a large bag filled with offerings and presents for those who have behaved throughout the year.

On Epiphany Eve, 5 January, La Befana makes her rounds. Those who have been good throughout the previous year receive gifts and sweets in their shoe or stocking, but those who haven't will find instead a lump of coal or 'dark candy', or a stick. It is common for people to leave offerings for her, usually consisting of a small plate of food and a glass of red wine.

Like Perchta, La Befana is also concerned with the state of people's houses. But in Befana's case, she lends a helping hand, and is said to sweep the floor or even tidy a little before she leaves. Some say this had a symbolic meaning, representing the sweeping away of problems and bad times.

The origin of the name La Befana is believed to be a corruption or mispronunciation of *epfania*, the Italian for Epiphany. Some link La Befana to Heria or Strenia – a pagan goddess who presided over New Year gifts.

There are several stories attached to La Befana. In one popular version, the Magi, following the star in search of the Messiah, come to see Befana on their journey. They ask her for directions to find the child but she doesn't know the way, instead giving them hospitality and shelter for the night. In gratitude, the next morning they ask her to go with them, but La Befana declines, unable to leave her household chores behind. Once they have departed, however, she regrets her choice, and sets off in search of them and the child. She is still searching to this day, and gives sweets or fruit to the good children that she finds along the way.

There are many variations of this tale, and in one La Befana sets out following the star laden with gifts, including baked items and a broom to clean for the new mother, Mary. In a sadder version, a grieving La Befana goes in search of the newborn, believing Jesus to be her own lost child. Upon finding him, she is consoled by being told she will be mother to all children from then on.

Although generally benign, be careful of upsetting La Befana: she likes to carry out her tasks unobserved. If she spies someone watching her, they can expect a thump on the shoulder with her broomstick as a light punishment.

Today, La Befana is hugely popular and is celebrated throughout Italy during Epiphany. The country's largest festival takes place in Urbania, from 2–6 January, and attracts around 40,000 visitors. La Befana arrives in a horse-drawn carriage, and children can visit the witch in her house, *La Casa della Befana*.

In Venice, 50 people dressed as La Befana take part in the *Regata della Befana*, a rowing race along the Grand Canal, while in Verona at the *rogo della vecia* – the burning of the old woman – a huge witch-figure puppet is set on fire before large crowds.

Sweet treats are closely associated with La Befana, and each region produces its own variety of goodies at this time of year. Among them, rum-flavoured biscuits known as *befami* are found in Tuscany, while from Piedmont *Fugassa d'la Befana* is a sweet focaccia bread with sugar and candied fruit.

Gryla

Another mis-identified witch, the Icelandic Gryla is not a witch at all, but a troll. This larger-than-life figure is said to live in a mountain cave during most of the year, but when it comes to Jól – the Christmas season – it is time to beware. For then Gryla ventures out in search of children who have misbehaved, a favourite ingredient in her stew or as a tasty snack.

The term Gryla was originally used to refer to all female trolls. In time, this came to stand for one female troll in particular, the figure we know today. In the oldest sources that mention her, Gryla roams around the countryside asking parents to give her their children who have misbehaved; giving her food or chasing her away could get rid of her instead.

Appearance-wise, there are varying descriptions of Gryla, but all agree that she is an enormous and terrifying figure. Some say she has 300 heads with three eyes each, while one description states she has an impressive 15 tails that hold 100 bags a piece: each bag in turn contains 20 children, destined for the stew pot. While the number of tails and bags varies, one thing is certain: it is best to keep out of her way!

Although Gryla was first mentioned in 13th-century texts as the personification of winter, she wasn't linked to Christmas specifically in written sources until the 17th century. Beginning life as a solitary figure, in later works Gryla was said to share her cave with her third husband, the lazy *Leppalúði*, and she is also said to be mother of Iceland's legendary Yule Lads. Completing the household is *Jólakötturinn* the Yule Cat, a huge and terrifying creature that prowls the countryside, eating anyone who hasn't been given new clothes before Christmas Eve.

Today, Gryla remains a force to be reckoned with as a cautionary tale to ensure good behaviour around the Christmas period. Belief in her is fierce, and many children are genuinely terrified of what she might do to them. Proof of Gryla's fame and importance is not hard to find; depictions of her abound across Iceland, including a statue at Keflavík airport.

PART TWO

The Witch Among Us: The Witch Trials and Beyond

Against a backdrop of religious, social and economic upheaval, the existence of witches and how to combat them became an issue of monumental importance across areas of Europe and the American colonies from the 15th to the 18th centuries. During this time, the witch became the ultimate enemy: the threat from within. Witches could be operating alone – mainly carrying out acts of *maleficia* such as bringing illness or death to people or livestock – or gathering in larger groups, becoming an endemic threat to society as a whole.

It is believed that between 40,000 and 60,000 individuals – women, men and children – were executed as witches during the period 1427–1782. As such estimates don't include those who fell foul of mob justice or the many who were found innocent and escaped with their lives, the total number of those accused of being a witch is much, much, higher.

The worst affected areas included southern Germany, Finnmark in Norway, and Scotland. Due to the use of torture to extract confessions and the work of overzealous 'witch hunters', several large-scale witch panics took place in these areas. A fatal snowballing of accusations and executions took place, with neighbour implicating neighbour, family and friends denouncing one another in turn to provide an ever-growing supply of fresh victims. Although the final death toll was less high in other areas of Europe such as England and also in the American Colonies, this doesn't diminish the atrocities that were carried out in these places, or the intensity of persecution that took place elsewhere.

Official prosecutions for witchcraft began to dwindle across Europe and America during the latter half of the 17th century, and with the dawning of the 18th century the spread of Enlightenment ideas meant belief in witchcraft and witches declined steadily among many of the educated elite. Although the last execution for witchcraft in Europe took place in 1782, it was not so easy to stem the tide among the general populace. Belief in witches and popular action against them continued well after the last trials were a distant memory, continuing in Europe and America well into the 20th century and beyond. In some areas of the world, persecution of supposed witches continues to this day, often with deadly consequences.

Thou Shalt Not Suffer a Witch To Live

From the 15th to the 18th centuries, witchcraft became a crime punishable by death. Executions took place in public before crowds of hundreds that turned out to witness the spectacle, with the last words of executed witches recorded and related in pamphlets, along with the grisly details of their many supposed crimes.

The majority of the total of those executed throughout this period were women, comprising 80–85 per cent of all victims. Along with being less financially and socially secure than men, popular belief stated that women were more likely to succumb to the Devil and his temptations due to their inherently weak and gullible nature, thus making them prime candidates for being accused of witchcraft. There were exceptions, however: records of men being named as witches are present across the majority of the areas where executions for witchcraft took place, and in Iceland, Estonia and Finland, 50 per cent or more of those accused of witchcraft were in fact men.

The most common method of execution for a convicted witch was that traditionally used for heretics: burning alive at the stake. Although for many, death was caused by smoke inhalation, this didn't save victims from the excruciating pain of heat and flames. In some areas of Germany, France and Scotland, sometimes the mercy of being strangled or hanged before burning was granted, but if the condemned later recanted their confession they would then be burned alive.

In England and America, convicted witches were generally hanged. In England, burning only occurred if the accused was also guilty of treason – against the monarch – or petty treason (against lord, master or husband), such as Mary Lakeland who was burned in Ipswich in 1645 for the crime of murdering her husband by witchcraft and convicted of several other witchcraft-related crimes and deaths.

Dispatching a witch was a costly business. Accounts from Aberdeen, Scotland, in 1597 record that 26 loads of peat, 6 loads of firewood, 4 barrels of tar, plus the transportation and setting up of the stake, cost £3 16s, plus a further 13s and 6d for the executioner's time and efforts. Hanging was substantially cheaper; to burn Mary Lakeland in 1645 cost Ipswich £3 3s 6d – three times what it would have cost to hang her.

Although the death toll is significant, the number of accused witches who went free is much larger. Of those who survived being labelled a witch, however, their 'freedom' was often in name only: the fates of such individuals included banishment, or, if allowed to return to their homes, they risked being ostracized, attacked and treated like criminals by neighbours, family and one-time friends alike.

The Hammer of Witches:
Malleus Maleficarum

Debate raged long and hard during the period of the witch trials regarding the nature of witchcraft and how exactly witches should be dealt with. Demonologists and scholars alike dedicated thousands of words to the subject, with books and pamphlets proliferating at a vast rate across Europe and beyond.

There is one book, however, that today stands out in the popular imagination above all others: *Malleus Maleficarum*, or 'The Hammer of Witches'. This vitriolic, misogynistic, and explicitly detailed text acted essentially as a witch hunter's handbook, and it has been described by some as the single most important publication regarding witches and witchcraft in history. But just what is this text and how influential has it been in the fight against witchcraft?

Written by Dominican inquisitor Heinrich Kramer, the *Malleus* was first published in 1486. The name of Jakob Sprenger was added to that of Kramer's in 1519, but there is ongoing debate regarding how much – if any – involvement Sprenger actually had.

The lengthy work is divided into multiple sections and chapters, each addressing different aspects of witchcraft, including the identification, prosecution and punishment of witches, detailed instructions for conducting witch trials, descriptions of supposed signs of witchcraft, and theological arguments supporting the persecution of witches. Impressively thorough, the book covers everything from how to question and torture suspects in order to extract the all-important confession, to the legalities of securing a conviction, and the book also served the purpose of spreading key ideas about witches that were to become firmly entrenched in witchcraft lore for decades to follow. It is from this text, for example, that the oft-cited idea of penis-stealing witches passed into popular discourse, along with many other descriptions highlighting the depravity and irredeemable nature of witches. As a testament to its popularity, the *Malleus* went through 26 editions between 1486 and 1600, and remains in print today.

Although the book is often said to be the greatest influence on the witch trials and singlehandedly responsible for the deaths of thousands, the truth is actually decidedly less dramatic. It has been noted by some scholars that there was no sudden escalation of trials and persecution after its publication, nor was there persecution in areas where there had been none previously. It has even been pointed out that in some areas there was a decrease in executions after the publication of the book. The *Malleus Maleficarum* was also condemned by leading theologians of the time for advocating procedures that were both illegal and unethical: in 1538 the Spanish Inquisition cautioned against taking the text at face value, especially some of the more obviously outlandish claims.

Some have suggested that the real power of the book lay in being a focus for debate and discussion surrounding the topic of witchcraft, and likewise as a basis for further ideas and arguments to be developed. This has done little to curb the notoriety of its reputation, and it remains a popular byword for the excesses of the witch trials today.

Baby Fat and Sex with Satan:
The Witches' Sabbath

The attendants riding flying goats, trampling the cross, and being re-baptized in the name of the Devil while giving their clothes to him, kissing his behind, and dancing back to back forming a round.

Compendium Maleficarum – Francesco Maria Guazzo, 1608

Starting in the 15th century and gathering hold in the decades that followed, the idea of witches gathering in large groups for nefarious purposes – often involving sex, the Devil and flying ointments made from the fat of unbaptized children – slowly but surely coalesced across much of Europe into the well-established trope of the Witches' Sabbath. The idea of such orgiastic gatherings, characterized by unbridled lust and renouncing of the Christian faith, was a deadly instrument in the hands of the authorities, and it was the snowballing of accusations from reports of the Sabbath – where one accused witch named several more who attended with her, who were then in turn brought in for questioning and then named others – that led to some of Europe's largest and most deadly witch trials of the Early Modern period.

Confessions of having attended a Sabbath can be found in trial documents and related records across northern Europe, and Sabbath narratives were particularly popular in Scotland and Germany, and across Sweden and Norway. Due to the more sparing use of torture in southern Europe, Sabbath accounts were less common in areas that fell under the jurisdiction of the Roman Inquisition, namely Italy, Spain and Portugal, and they were also uncommon in Dutch, Hungarian, Danish and English cases.

Accounts of the Sabbath were far from uniform, with details varying across time and place. Although the writings of Early Modern demonologists were filled with titillating accounts of the Sabbath as little more than depraved sexual orgies, a rather different picture is painted in the confessions of the accused witches themselves. It is generally accepted that interrogators shaped confessions to fit what they wanted to hear, and the use of torture casts doubt on the veracity of much that was said under such conditions. There has been a more recent recognition, however, that the accused themselves did in fact have some input into and influence over how accounts of the Sabbath were recorded, helping to shape and form the narrative that resulted.

In many areas, the Sabbath was described as being closer to a party or social occasion than a meeting of murderous, bloodthirsty witches, and festive gatherings involving eating and dancing were particularly common across Norway, Sweden and Denmark. In accounts from Finnmark, Norway, dancing was the most prominent Sabbath activity: in 1663 Solve Nilsdatter recounted how another woman named Lirren was dancing with the Devil so enthusiastically she wore right through the sole of her shoe. When she complained, it was said that the Devil graciously gave her a replacement. The Sabbath in Hungary was likewise described in terms more suggestive of a community gathering than a demonic spectacle, and Sabbath accounts from Scotland also tended towards singing and dancing.

Feasting was also a common theme in many descriptions of the Sabbath. A preoccupation with food by people who all too often went without is illustrative, as it indicates a certain amount of wish-fulfilment entering the narrative. In 17th-century Zagreb, Croatia, Jela Magdalenika told of how when witches met they feasted on half-cooked red meat, cooked roast veal and pork, and drank wine, both mulled and cold.
In Scotland, feasting likewise featured prominently and the food was again much better than those confessing would have been used to, with accounts filled with good food, meat and wine, in stark contrast to the predominantly grain-based diet and ale that would have been their reality.

Sabbath accounts were not confined to adults: evidence from children was not uncommon, and there was a distinct increase in Sabbath accounts by children towards the end of the 17th century. In 1630, nine-year-old Christine Teipel of Obenkirchen, Germany, described how she had flown to a gathering of witches with the aid of ointment rubbed under her arms. She also related how she had met with witches on a mountain top – there the Devil distributed fine clothing to those gathered, and they drank wine and beer from golden barrels. During the severe witch panic in Würzburg, Germany, during the 1620s, around 160 people were executed between 1627 and 1629, largely as a result of children testifying that they and others had attended the Sabbath.

Overall, many Sabbath accounts seem to echo celebrations that accused witches might have attended within their communities, albeit in some cases with embellished details of what they would like to have experienced. There were some notable exceptions: far from being an expression of wish-fulfilment, Sabbath accounts from Lorraine, France, generally followed the same restrictive hierarchy that governed everyday life. One confession described how the officers – usually male – and other male witches flew off to do damage to crops, while the women stayed behind at the Sabbath site to cook and await their return. The witches of Lorraine were again short-changed in their Sabbath fare: the food was said to taste bad and was unsalted.

Due to their isolated locations, mountains featured heavily as a gathering place for witches in both legends and confessions alike. One of the most famous of these was The Brocken, or Blocksberg, in northern Germany, which was mentioned frequently in accounts of the Sabbath from not only Germany itself but also across the Nordic countries, especially Sweden and Denmark. Lyderhorn was another well-known 'witch mountain', located near Bergen on the west coast of Norway. In 1590 Anne Pedersdatter, wife of a prominent minister, confessed that she had joined other witches for gatherings there for three Christmas Eves in a row.

In Iceland, Hekla – one of the country's most active volcanoes – was closely connected to witchcraft and the supernatural. Known in the Middle Ages as the Gateway to Hell, in the wake of an eruption in 1341 birds were seen flying in the fire; these were thought to be souls of the dead, further cementing a reputation that persisted until the 19th century. Hekla features in trial accounts from Norway and Denmark, and witches from Finnmark were also said to have travelled there. Hekla was also said to have been the prison of Judas Iscariot after his betrayal of Jesus.

Blåkulla, or Blue Hill, was a legendary island where the Devil was said to hold court during the Sabbath. This location was of particular importance during the Mora witch trials in Sweden of 1668–76, where it became a feature of many confessions, and many witches described a vast meadow of which it was impossible to see the far side and a house where witches would meet the Devil for a meal and general rowdiness. Reaching Blåkulla was only possible via magical flight: witches were said to ride a variety of items including goats, horses, fence posts and spits in order to meet there.

Today, the riding of witches to Blåkulla near Easter is remembered in the tradition of Easter Witches: in Sweden, on Maundy Thursday or Easter Saturday, young children go door to door, dressed in long skirts with aprons, scarves about their heads, and freckles painted on their faces. They offer those inside drawings and in return are given sweets or sometimes small amounts of money. Known as *påskkärring*, meaning Easter Witch or Easter Hag, this tradition stems from the belief that on Maundy Thursday witches flew from Sweden to Blåkulla for a Sabbath with the Devil, before returning home again on Easter Eve. There is a similar tradition in Finland: in western Finland, young witches are said to be abroad on Easter Sunday, while for those in the rest of the country the Sunday before – Palm Sunday – is the day of choice.

Although some witches travelled great distances, many Sabbaths took place much closer to home. In Denmark, witches often gathered to meet with the Devil in their local churches. In Scotland, witches also tended to stay local, meeting in places within easy reach of where they lived: local kirkyards were common locations, as were hills and moors in the vicinity. Witches also gathered in each other's homes, with several confessions including such meetings. Local crossroads or gallows were also popular there, and this was also the case in central southeastern Europe; such boundaries were liminal spaces, associated with magic and the supernatural.

Travelling to and from the Sabbath could be a complex affair. Scottish witches rarely gave information on how they arrived at Sabbaths; because places were so close to home, it was generally accepted that they went on foot. There were, however, some occasions where transport was mentioned; Agnes Sampson and Geillis Duncan said that they arrived at the meeting of the North Berwick witches on horseback. Witches were also claimed to travel in boats shaped like chimneys, in sieves, and in some cases confessed that that they were carried to the Sabbath on the back of their fellow witches. In Zagreb, Croatia, the Devil was said to transport his witches to and from the Sabbath in his coach pulled by six black horses.

Almost universally, the Sabbath took place under cover of darkness, reinforcing the picture of clandestine, ungodly gatherings. Despite the late hour, however, witches could not always guarantee slipping away undetected. In some accounts, in order not to arouse suspicion, an accused witch claimed to have left a substitute in their bed so their absence would not be noted. Scottish witch Isobel Gowdie recounted how she and her fellow witches left a charmed broom in this fashion, which took on the form of a sleeping woman to observers.

Fabricated fantasies regarding marginalized groups meeting in secret for lewd and perverted purposes were common long before the witch trials: early Christians, Jews, the Cathars and the Knights Templar were among those who had previously received similar treatment, with devastating consequences. Witches therefore were in many ways just the next in line in a well-established system used to besmirch, discredit and 'otherize' those who were viewed with suspicion and distrust.

For many, Sabbath tales were accepted at face value, proof of the terrible deeds carried out by witches. Early critics disputed this, however, taking such accounts as proof instead of the delusion that those confessing were under, maintaining that the Sabbath was all just part of an illusion created by the Devil to fool the gullible and impressionable.

The concept of the Sabbath has been hotly debated; over the

centuries, there have been many theories put forward regarding whether witches did indeed attend any sort of gathering and, if so, what form this took. A recent idea that has gained popularity is that details of some confessions were actually part of real, visionary experiences. According to Emma Wilby, Scottish witches actually attended the Sabbath, albeit in a visionary sense, with links to shamanic practices and dream cults that she believes may have been in existence in Scotland in the Early Modern period.

Apart from a smattering of cases during the 1645 East Anglian witch hunts and other isolated incidents, ideas of the Sabbath were almost entirely absent from English witchcraft trials. It is not a surprise therefore to find no traces initially of the Sabbath across the Atlantic in New England. In 1692, however, with the advent of the Salem witch trials, the idea of witches gathering together to plan their evil deeds became part of the official narrative, and this idea was in part responsible for the swift spread of persecution there. Instead of being referred to as Sabbaths, Salem witches were said to gather for 'meetings', reflecting the name given to the Sunday church services. Salem witches didn't attend their gatherings in person and were instead there in spectral form: invisible, only fellow witches or those bewitched by them could see those in attendance. There was no talk of orgies or ointments at these meetings – witches in Salem gathered strictly to gain instruction from their Satanic leader. Meeting in the field next door to the minister's house, these audacious witches feasted on red bread and wine, both of which were said to contain blood.

In the Devil's Name

The Devil, believed by the Early Modern Church to be the root of all evil, was inextricably linked to the story of the witch.

According to confessions, he would appear to an individual unexpectedly, at a point where they were most vulnerable: whether due to extreme poverty, hunger or desperation, or in the grip of strong emotions such as loneliness, anger or jealousy. The Devil, preying on such weakness, was quick to offer not only a sympathetic ear, but also money and, most crucially for many, the means to take revenge on those who had wronged them. All that was required in return was to renounce God, give up their soul, and follow the Devil as their Lord and Master. Once agreement was obtained, the deal was sealed variously by the Devil marking his newly created witch, the signing of a physical pact – often with the witch's own blood – writing their name in the Devil's book, and sexual intercourse.

The manner in which the Devil helped the witch to get her own back on those who had wronged her varied. One common method was through a white powder that the witch was instructed to use on her victim. Sticks were also popular; Catherine la Rondelatte of Lorraine confessed she was given a stick and told that she could harm people she disliked or their animals simply by touching them with it. Mengeotte Gascon was given a powder, but was also told that simply striking someone with her hand could be used to either harm or kill.

As was to be expected, however, the Devil proved to be a duplicitous sort, and his promises and honeyed words meant precious little, as many witches discovered to their cost. Often, the money given to them turned to leaves or dung soon after, and where real money was received, it was usually only for a brief period and a mere fraction of the riches that were initially promised. The Devil was also known to make promises of protection and freedom from detection which he likewise invariably reneged on, deserting the witch in prison or at the gallows in her very hour of need.

There are varying descriptions of what the Devil looked like. In many confessions he appeared in the form of a man: according to an account of a Sabbath from the Mora trials in Sweden, the Devil appeared 'in a gray coat, and red and blue stockings: he had a red beard, a high crowned hat, with linen of diverse colours, wrapped about it, and long garters upon his stockings.'

Confessing witches often described the Devil as a man dressed in black. In 1634, Margaret Johnson from Lancashire described how the Devil came to her as a man in a black suit and offered her food and also revenge against her enemies in exchange for her soul. The Devil could appear as varying heights; some stated that he was tall, while others related a man of middling stature. In many accounts, the Devil was described as attractive and good-looking. According to Rebecca West of Lawford, Essex, the Devil appeared as a young man one night in her room as she was going to bed. Handsome and irresistible, he promised to be her loving husband until death and to bring revenge to her enemies. Elizabeth or Bess Clarke of Manningtree, Essex, the first woman persecuted by the self-styled Witchfinder General Matthew Hopkins, described the Devil as a 'tall, proper, black-haired gentleman'. He was, she finished triumphantly, a far better gentleman than the Witchfinder himself.

Sex with the Devil was a mainstay of demonological fantasies, and this detail likewise entered into some confessions.

Those who admitted to a physical relationship with the Devil frequently reported that he was unnaturally cold; descriptions such as 'lips cold as clay' and lying heavy and cold atop a confessing witch were common. Accused witches often revealed that they knew the identity of the handsome visitor by the fact that, despite his human appearance, a cloven foot was visible beneath his clothes. When he spoke, many said that the Devil had a 'hollow' voice, again highlighting the supernatural nature of their visitor.

Some witches even confessed to marrying the Devil or being his wife. Margaret Wyard of Suffolk related how the Devil came to her as a handsome young man with yellow hair and black clothes, saying that he was her husband. Although not common, it was possible for a witch to become pregnant by the Devil. According to one source, when the Devil at Blåkulla had intercourse with his favourite witches, these couplings brought forth sons and daughters who, in turn, then mated with each other – the result was offspring of serpents and toads.

The Devil could also present himself in animal form. In Salem, the Devil came to Reverend Parris's enslaved servant, Tatabe or Tituba, in the form of a hog, and then as a great black dog, which ordered her to serve him and harm the children who were believed to be bewitched. According to Anne Lauritsdatter of Finnmark, the Devil was hairy and had horns, likewise implying a creature rather than a man, and in confessions from some areas the Devil was reported in the form of a goat.

In 1584, Margaret Cooper of Ditcheat, Somerset, England, recounted how she had been rolled down the stairs by the Devil while he tormented her; he was in the form of a headless bear.

In many Sabbath accounts from Finnmark, the Devil's primary function appeared to be entertainment. According to Margrette Jonsdatter, at a Sabbath on Mount Domen on St John's Eve, Satan played the fiddle for those assembled while they danced and drank wine and beer. He was also known on occasion to participate in board games. Likewise in Scotland, the Devil was prone to playing music, and danced and feasted with the assembled witches rather than taking a leading role. The ability to play a variety of instruments was also ascribed to him: the most common was a fiddle – more specifically in some accounts, such as those from the 1662–63 Finnmark trials, a red one – that he would play while the witches danced merrily. In some accounts, he was said to have played the *langeleik* – a Norwegian stringed instrument, played flat on the ground – and a *lur*, a long natural blowing horn made of wood and wrapped in birch. At Blåkulla, it was said that the Devil played the harp before taking his favourites to bed.

More in keeping with his general reputation, the Devil could and did incite witches to acts of malevolence. Although not a primary factor in Scottish cases, in the North Berwick trials of 1590, the accused witches were famously said to have raised storms while King James was at sea, and in 1662 Isobel Gowdie described many times when she and fellow witches planned to kill and maim with the Devil's help, including acts such as destruction of crops, livestock and ships.

Once an individual promised themselves to the Devil, it was nigh on impossible to get free again. In 1602, Catherine Charpentier of Remémont, France, confessed to a friar at St Nicholas of how she had fallen prey to the Devil and his promises. When told that she should carry with her holy bread and candle wax and confess to her own local priest the following Easter however, she found herself unable to confess due to the guilt and fear she felt. According to Charpentier, the Devil leapt at the opportunity and quickly reclaimed her for his own.

From Midsummer to Halloween:
When Witches Meet

Humankind has long attached significance to specific dates, and certain times of the year came to be associated with witchcraft and magic. Although the 'when' of the Sabbath was not of particular interest to interrogators, it's interesting that some confessing witches voluntarily provided details of exactly when the gatherings they attended took place. It is therefore possible to identify which dates were particularly important on a personal level, and which times of year were significantly associated with witchcraft and the supernatural within a community.

Many Sabbaths were said to have taken place on or close to a major annual festival. In Scandinavian countries, the night before Easter was closely associated with the gathering of witches, while in some areas of central southeastern Europe, Christmas Eve or the night before was a popular gathering time.

The night of 23–24 June – commonly known today as Midsummer's Eve or St John's Eve – was another customary time named for Sabbath gatherings, and an important date in general throughout Europe, closely associated with witchcraft and magic. During the Finnmark trials of 1620–21, Marrite Olufsdatter confessed that one year a group of witches including herself met in the air high above the mountains on that night. Likewise, in 1662–63, Margrette Jonsdatter confessed that she went to the Domen – a bare, flat-topped mountain in eastern Finnmark – with other witches on St John's Eve, where she danced and drank beer and wine.

Walpurgis Nacht, also known as St Walpurga's Eve, took place on 30 April, and was another popular meeting date for witches across northern and central Europe. It was a night when it was believed that evil spirits were strong, and bonfires were lit to give protection to people and animals.

According to confessions, the main dates for Scottish witches to meet were the four cross-quarter days of Candlemas (2 February), Beltane (1 May), Lammas (1 August) and Halloween (31 October) – all dates with a close association with the supernatural and witch and fairy lore in particular. Other dates mentioned in confessions were Rood Day/Holy Cross Day, Andrewmas, Whitsuntide and Pasche or Easter, all significant secular or religious celebrations in Scotland. This suggests that the witches deliberately chose dates for their gatherings that already had a known connection to the supernatural or importance in their own lives.

In southeastern Europe, other dates mentioned for Sabbath gatherings included St Elijah's Day (20 July), while some witches in Herzegovina said that they went to the Sabbath on St Jevdokija's Day (14 March), St Joachim and Anna's Day (26 July) and the autumn equinox (on or around 22 September).

Taking to the Skies:
Witches and Broomsticks

Ask anyone today how witches travel and chances are they will tell you, 'on a broomstick'. But has it always been so, and where does this association come from?

Witches during ancient times were not particularly renowned for flying, and it was not until the 15th century that this connection began to appear in witchcraft-related belief and folklore. There are many confessions from this time involving witches flying astride various items, such as a shovel, distaff, pitchfork or even a piece of straw. But ultimately the broom – a traditional symbol of female domesticity – won out, and quickly became the transport of choice according to accusers and confessing witches themselves.

The first known printed image of a witch astride a broom comes from *Hexenflug der Vaudoises* (Flight of the Witches) a miniature from Martin le Franc's 1451 *Le Champion des Dames*. A female figure wearing a headscarf is clearly flying astride a broom, while another is flying on a wooden staff just beneath her.

The first recorded confession to riding on a broom in connection with witchcraft was in 1453. Guillaume Edelin, Prior of St Germain en Laye near Paris, found himself under scrutiny after preaching a sermon against the reality of the Witches' Sabbath. Edelin was arrested, and under torture confessed to honouring the Devil – in the form of a ram or sheep – and kissing him on the buttocks. According to Edelin, the Devil would give him his help whenever he needed it, in exchange for always being at his beck and call. When the Devil wanted him, all Edelin needed to do was stand astride a broom and he would be transported to his new master instantly. He was said to have a written copy of the contract he had signed with the Devil on him when he was arrested, further compounding his guilt.

Edelin confessed and repented on a scaffold in the city of Evreux, where he was publicly chastised for his many sins. Some sources say he was executed afterwards; in actuality he was spared, but died later in prison.

There was much contemporary debate surrounding whether a witch physically engaged in flight, or whether they instead fell into a trance or drugged state, brought on by the hallucinogenic properties of the 'flying ointment' that became increasingly popular in demonological writings from the 15th century onwards. Suggested ingredients of this ointment included belladonna, henbane, poppy, wolfsbane, hemlock and bat's blood, not forgetting the ubiquitous fat of dead infants.

Some sources stated that the witch anointed herself with the ointment – sometimes all over, sometimes as a lubricant in the genital area – while others believed that the witch instead rubbed the ointment into the object she used for flight. Some said that the ointment wasn't actually necessary at all; instead, with its list of disturbing and evocative ingredients, it stood simply as a cipher for the inherent depravity of the witch.

Pricking and Swimming:
A Discovery of Witches

Suspecting a person of witchcraft was one thing, but how was it possible to find proof in order to bring them to justice? Various methods of discovery developed over the period of the witch trials, used alike by those in authority, by self-professed witchfinders who travelled from place to place rooting out witches, and by neighbours.

Swimming a Witch

One of the most popular ways of identifying a witch was to 'swim' them. Although finer details could vary, the basic premise was as follows: the suspected witch was bound – right thumb to left big toe and vice versa – and thrown or lowered into a body of water such as a lake or pond or even, in the case of Finnmark, the sea. If they sank, they were innocent, and would hopefully be pulled out before they drowned. If they floated on the surface of the water, however, they were a witch and guilty.

Often, the suspect was introduced to the water not once, but three times, just to be on the safe side.

The idea of testing for innocence by water was not without precedent. Use of ordeal by water was present in the ancient law codes; according to the second law of the Babylonian Code of Hammurabi a man was to leap into a river if accused of a crime by another. If he survived, he was innocent, and the person accusing him would be put to death, while the accused inherited his house. In England, between 1166 and 1215, a version of swimming was used to try felony pleas. Here, however, it was reserved until after a guilty verdict had already been reached: the method was short-lived, banned by the Fourth Lateran Council.

Swimming of suspected witches became common practice across Europe during the late 16th and 17th centuries, and was particularly prevalent in German cases. James VI of Scotland (later James I of England) furthered its popularity and usage by advocating the approach in his *Daemonologie* of 1597, as did the pamphlet account of one of the earliest cases of swimming in England, that of Mother Sutton in Bedfordshire. Despite being endorsed by the king, interestingly, swimming was noticeably absent from Scottish cases.

Swimming was not an officially sanctioned practice, and was usually carried out by members of the community in an attempt to confirm guilt before legal proceedings were set in motion. This left a great deal of room for error and abuse, and swimming was frowned upon by many in authority, leading to its eventual ban in England in 1645 due largely to the excessive usage of this method by Matthew Hopkins. In France, the swimming of witches was likewise forbidden from the mid-17th century and it was also banned in Germany. Despite this, the practice continued unofficially in these countries until well into the 19th century in many areas.

Swimming was not a gentle process by any stretch of the imagination; freezing water temperatures, combined with rough handling and violence by overzealous locals, meant it was fraught with danger, and even if an individual sank and was technically found innocent, this was no guarantee of safety. It was not uncommon for the suspected witch to drown during the ordeal, or to survive, only to perish from the cold afterwards. In 1751 in Tring, Hertfordshire, Ruth and John Osborne were seized by a mob and taken to a nearby pool. Wearing only a sheet, the elderly and frail Ruth was bound at her wrists and feet and forced into the water, where she was dragged from bank to bank by a rope and prodded with a stick to force her under the water. Unsurprisingly, she did not survive: although subjected to the same treatment, her husband, miraculously, made it out alive. Despite the known dangers, however, some individuals willingly agreed to be swum or even, in some cases, asked for the process to be carried out in the hope of clearing their names and bringing an end to the unbearable persecution they endured.

Witch swimming was particularly slow to die out, and some countries, such as Poland, experienced swimming or dunking of suspected witches well into the 19th century and perhaps even longer. As time went on, however, it became increasingly likely that those who carried out a swimming would face repercussions; the man mainly responsible for swimming Ruth Osborne was hanged, and a group responsible for the death of the individual known as Dummy in Essex in 1863 were likewise dealt with harshly by the authorities.

Witch Pricking

When a witch promised themselves to the Devil, it was said that they were given a physical mark. According to popular belief, such marks were insensible to pain and would not bleed, even when pricked with a sharp object. The idea behind pricking a witch was simple yet deadly: if a mark was pricked and the suspect didn't show pain, then they were guilty.

Although a seemingly straightforward method of determining guilt, in practice, the process was fraught with problems. Quick to capitalize on the idea, professional 'witch prickers' soon started to appear, offering their 'expert' services to root out witches in an area. Working for a fee, it was in the best interests of the pricker to identify as many witches as possible, leaving room for any number of abuses. Tales abound of retractable bodkins or needles, where the point retreated inside the base when pressed against a suspect, or of a method where the blunt end of the implement was pressed against the mark, before quickly turning it round so that those watching – the victim included – would think that the sharp end had been used. Of course, the accused would feel no pain, and another 'witch' would be successfully uncovered.

The pricking process was neither a quick nor a comfortable one. In front of a watching crowd, a suspect would be stripped and shaved completely, before being subjected to every inch of flesh being investigated. Any mark or blemish down to the slightest discoloration was considered suspect, and each was pricked in turn, sometimes several times just to make certain, the witch watched closely for any sign of reaction. It was all too easy for the suspected witch – naked, terrified, potentially sleep deprived, and under the barrage of noise and bustle all around – to become confused and disoriented. In such a state, their senses and reactions dulled, any hint that pain had not been felt was readily leapt upon, taken as evidence of guilt.

In England, pricking was used extensively by Matthew Hopkins and fellow witchfinder John Stearne during the 1640s, and it was also present in the trials of the Pendle Witches in Lancashire in 1612. It was in Scotland, however, that pricking was particularly prevalent; across that country there were approximately ten known prickers during the 17th century, mostly active from around 1648 until 1662. The evidence obtained by these individuals was used to secure the conviction and execution of many of the approximately two thousand executed for witchcraft across Scotland.

The most famous of the Scottish prickers was John Kincaid. Although based in Lothian, Kincaid travelled much further afield, and was instrumental in securing convictions in several of the major witch hunts. Scottish prickers were also known to be invited into counties in the north of England; one such pricker was paid 20 shillings per witch detected in Newcastle in 1649. Kincaid was exposed as fraudulent in 1662 and, after being imprisoned, confessed to his lies. It is thought that his arrest and that of fellow pricker John Dick played a significant part in the practice of witch pricking eventually being abolished.

Although pricking was a man's job, there is some evidence of the existence of at least two female prickers. One of these, Christian Caddell, dressed as a man and under the assumed name of John Dickson began pricking witches in Elgin, Moray, in March 1662, working for John Innes, the Baillie of Spynie. Her true identity was revealed when she was imprisoned just over a year later due to complaints about her conduct; she was sentenced to transportation to Barbados and her ultimate fate is unknown.

Searching for Teats

Sometimes conflated with or confused with the witch's mark, witches were believed to have a special teat or nipple from which they fed their familiars. Michael Dalton, in *The Country Justice*, counselled that a test for discovering a witch was to look for a teat in an unusual place on the body where a familiar would be suckled.

Female searchers were employed to look for such evidence, and witch hunters such as Hopkins and Stearne often had one or more in their retinue as they travelled from place to place. Such teats were often in private places, and many were said to be in or near the suspect's genitals. Other locations for teats included on the head or thighs, under the tongue, or on or by the witch's fingers. Teats could vary in size and were not always visible: Bridget Bishop of Salem was said to have a small teat, but it was gone when searched for again a few hours later.

After Alice Samuel of Warboys was hanged for witchcraft in 1593, her body was searched by the jailer and his wife and a teat discovered 'adjoining so secret a place which was not decent to be seen'. A little lump of flesh, 1.25cm (0.5in) long, this teat was shown to many people as proof that Samuel had indeed been a witch. According to accounts, when the gaoler's wife squeezed it with her hand, 'a mixture of yellowish milk and water issued out of it, then clear milk, and at last, blood itself'.

Waking and Walking

It was not just physical signs that were necessary to condemn a witch, and great lengths were taken to extract a confession from the accused. It became quickly apparent that a confused, sleep-deprived suspect would more readily agree to what questioners wanted, and keeping the accused awake until they confessed to their supposed crimes became a popular method of establishing guilt.

In England, where torture was legally prohibited, waking became particularly popular, and, despite his later protestations to the contrary, was used extensively by Matthew Hopkins in his reign of terror across East Anglia. Delirious through lack of sleep, the accused could be made to confess to almost anything: one woman from Suffolk, deprived of food and rest, confessed to having an imp called Nan. Luckily for her, a local gentleman intervened, sent the watchers away and let the woman eat and sleep: upon recovering, the woman had no idea as to what she had confessed, and it turned out that 'Nan' was the name she sometimes used for a chicken she owned.

Keeping someone awake for a long stretch of time was not as easy as it sounds, and there were various methods employed to keep the suspect from sleeping. A suspect could be made to sit cross-legged on a stool or table, relentlessly prodded awake if they started to droop. Even in areas such as Germany where torture was legally permissible, sleep deprivation was still a popular aid to extracting a confession and could be aided by the use of terrible instruments: in some places, an iron bridle would be fitted around the suspect's head and attached to the wall with a short chain. They would then be unable to sit or lie down, forced to stay awake until they confessed to what was required of them.

Another popular way to ensure that a witch couldn't sleep was to walk them. The accused would be made to walk back and forth across the room, over and over, often led or held forcibly so they had no choice but to move. Brutally effective, a worn out and bloodied victim would often confess out of sheer exhaustion: 80-year-old Reverend John Lowes of Brandeston, Suffolk, was walked and kept awake for several days and nights before finally, almost insensible, confessing to the accusations against him, including bewitching cattle, killing many by sinking a ship off Harwich harbour, murdering Mary Cooke and many others by witchcraft, and having six imps or familiars that he conferred with daily in order to commit his crimes. Despite recanting his confession once recovered, Lowes was executed on 27 August 1645, still protesting his innocence.

One of the last recorded instances of walking being used to extract a confession in England was that of widowed Rachel Chambers, from Ubbeston, Suffolk, in 1693. She confessed after being walked to murdering her husband and the Lady Blois through witchcraft, even though the relatives of the dead woman believed her death to be from natural causes. Chambers died in Beccles prison before she could come to trial.

Weighing against the Bible

One of the easiest tests to 'pass' was that of being weighed against the church Bible. The accused – often naked – would be placed in one side of the scale, and the Bible in the other. If the witch was lighter than the Bible, then they were guilty. If they were heavier, which in most cases they were – in the first attested case of weighing a witch in England, the bible weighed about 5.44kg (12lb), and in general church Bibles tended to weigh at a maximum 10kg (22lb), the weight of a one-year-old boy – then they were innocent.

Weighing against the Bible was a particularly popular method of proving a witch in England and North America during the 18th and 19th centuries, and was often carried out after, or in place of, being swum. Weighing a witch was also one of the more humane methods of identification compared with others, and although it was potentially practised earlier, it didn't come to the forefront of witchcraft cases until many of the other, more violent, tests had been discontinued.

The first attested case of weighing a witch against the Bible in England is from Oakley, Bedfordshire, in 1737, but it is highly likely that that it was a known practice from at least the mid-17th century. In 1780 in Bexhill, locals asked a local clergyman to weigh two women they suspected of witchcraft. The women proved to be heavier than the book, thus satisfying their accusers. In June 1792, an elderly woman from Stanningfield, Suffolk, was so fed up with being persecuted that she asked to be weighed in order to clear her name. When this was refused she agreed to being swum instead, a process that nearly killed her but, thankfully, proved her innocence when she duly sank.

The idea of being weighed against the Bible is often confused with another similar, yet distinctly separate, practice found in northern Europe. Individuals that had been slandered by accusations of witchcraft would go to a weigh house and ask to be weighed: if their actual weight was in keeping with how heavy their appearance suggested, a certificate would then be issued stating that they were of 'normal weight'. One of the most well-known weigh houses was in Oudewater, Netherlands, and was used for this purpose until the 1720s; weighing also took place in nearby Utrecht and in Bocholt, in modern-day Germany.

It was no simple matter to be weighed: at Oudewater, permission had to be obtained from the city officials. Women coming to be weighed would be helped to undress by a midwife, while men were seen to by the sheriff's officer: the individual would then be searched for any items concealed about their body to purposefully influence their weight. With women clad only in a shift and undergarment – though from 1710 they were covered with a long black cloak – and men wearing only a shirt, they would then be weighed by two aldermen and other attending notables and the verdict recorded. Although not legally binding and recording only that the individual was of normal weight rather than that they were innocent of witchcraft, the certificates issued were highly regarded due to the influence they had over local opinion.

What both weighing practices have in common is that they operated on the generally held belief that witches were lighter than normal humans. The origins of this idea may have been linked to the fact that witches flew to the Sabbath and were therefore supernaturally light, or the belief that their lack of soul in turn made them lighter than usual.

Touch Test

As the name suggests, this method of witch identification involved the suspect coming into physical contact with one or more of their supposed victims. Such touching could be carried out in a variety of ways and could be intentional or unintentional, but the outcome was the same: proving the guilt or otherwise of the accused.

One common method was to have the bewitched victim – usually in the throes of a fit and thus deemed insensible – placed in a room. One at a time, potential suspects would be brought in and instructed to touch the victim. In many cases, the victim would appear to just 'know' when they were touched by the 'witch', at which point they would cry out against them, their torments increasing visibly. In 1662, Rose Cullender and Amy Denny were accused of bewitching two young girls. In their fits, the girls' fists clenched tightly and couldn't be opened even when others tried to force them apart. In court, they opened their hands only when Rose Cullender touched them, seeming to prove her guilt. In 1712 in Walkern, Hertfordshire, in an attempt to clear her name, elderly Jane Wenham named several other women as having bewitched the maid Anne Thorn. Unfortunately for Wenham, when they were brought one at a time to the suffering young woman she showed no sign of recognizing their presence. It was only when Jane herself was brought in that Anne 'flew up with great strength and fury' and demanded to know why Jane had come to torment her again, further confirming the suspicions against her.

Whether evidence from this method was taken as solid proof of guilt or not depended on the situation and the credulity of the witnesses and officials involved. In several cases, particularly when the victim of supposed witchcraft reacted in the same manner regardless of who was brought before them, deception was easily uncovered, and many a fraud was exposed in such a way. Sometimes such obvious fakery was dismissed, however: in the case of Cullender and Denny, when one of the girls had an apron put in front of her face, she opened her hands when touched by another individual, leading some observers to declare that the girls were fabricating their condition. Tragically, this wasn't considered enough proof of innocence and the two women were subsequently hanged.

Another popular belief was that if a murderer touched the corpse of one of their victims, it would bleed. In 1608, Jennet Preston from Gisburn-on-Craven, Lancashire, was suspected of murdering her employer Thomas Lister by witchcraft. It was said that when she touched his body, fresh blood issued forth, thus confirming suspicions held by his son and others that she was responsible for his death. Jennet was tried in 1612 due to her links with the Pendle Witches and was found guilty of murdering Thomas Lister; she was hanged at York on 29 July 1612.

Reciting the Lord's Prayer

It was a generally accepted belief that a witch was unable to say certain holy words. Instructing a suspected witch to recite the Lord's Prayer became a popular test, and making a mistake was taken as further proof that the individual was a witch. While such evidence wasn't enough to secure a conviction on its own, it served as good supporting evidence that the suspect was indeed guilty.

Although a seemingly easy test to pass, this was not always the case. Terrified and under great scrutiny, it was all too easy for a suspect to muddle their words or omit parts of the prayer in their distressed state. In 1596, Alice Gooderidge from Stapenhill, Staffordshire, couldn't repeat 'and lead us not into temptation' along with other parts of the prayer, which was seen to confirm her guilt. Jane Wenham likewise failed to say the prayer on several occasions. She left out 'Forgive us our trespasses' and said 'Lead us not into no temptation' when ordered to recite the prayer by the Reverend Strutt, vicar of Ardeley. Even after practising, the next day she still could not get it right, and it was after this final failure that she confessed to the accusations against her.

On the scaffold itself, Alice Samuel of Warboys was asked to say the prayer; she stumbled on the words 'but deliver us from evil', which was taken as further proof that her impending death was justified. Even being able to say the prayer didn't guarantee freedom: George Burroughs of Salem recited it word perfect from the gallows in August 1692, but his ability to do so was interpreted as a trick of the Devil, and he was hanged regardless.

Making a Witch Cake

The precise origins of this intriguing method of witch detection are shrouded in mystery, with even the details of the practice not always clear, as they varied from place to place. The basic idea was as follows: urine from the bewitched victim was mixed with flour – and sometimes other ingredients – before being made into a cake and cooked over a fire. The resulting mixture could then be variously buried, burned or fed to an animal, in order to either reveal the identity of the witch or to break their hold over a victim.

In King's Lynn, Norfolk, at some point prior to 1617, the widowed Elizabeth Hancocke was wrongly accused by Mary Smith of stealing one of her chickens. When Hancocke confronted Smith and took her to task for making such accusations, Smith retaliated by wishing 'the pox to light upon her' and called Hancocke names. A few hours after this altercation, Hancocke fell ill. When her condition continued for over three weeks, her father consulted a wizard or cunning man who showed him the face of the witch responsible in a glass and gave him the following recipe:

Flour to be mixed with patient's own water [urine] and baked on the hearth, one half to be applied to the region of the heart, the other half to the back. The cake to be first spread with an ointment like treacle, a powder to be cast upon it, and certain words written in a paper.

In this instance at least, such actions were believed to be successful as the ill woman recovered, and the hold of the witch was said to have been broken – only for Hancocke to relapse at a future point after her new husband rashly killed Smith's cat.

Another example comes from the diary of the Reverend Oliver Haywood of Yorkshire. An entry for 1688 relates how the troubled mother of an ill child visited him to ask for his advice. A variety of doctors had been unable to help her 12-year-old son, and a friend had brought another doctor to try and ease his suffering. This doctor declared the boy 'hurt by an evil tongue' and refused to treat him until his urine had been tried by fire, instructing the mother to then 'make a cake or loaf of it, with wheat meal and put some of his hair into it and horseshoe stumps and then put it in the fire'. Troubled, the mother wanted to know whether it was wise to follow this suggestion – the reverend, after consulting with another minister from the area, concluded that as the practice had no foundation in either nature or the Bible then it was not of God and should therefore not be attempted.

Perhaps the most famous example of a witch cake comes from 1692 at the very start of the Salem witch trials. Betty Parris, the Reverend Parrises' daughter, and her cousin Abigail Williams started experiencing attacks from an unseen force. Neighbour Mary Sibley asked the Parris's enslaved servant known as 'John Indian' to make a witch cake. The girls' urine was duly mixed with flour and baked, before being fed to the family dog. When this act came to light, the Reverend Parris was horrified, identifying the creation of the witch cake as witchcraft itself: 'going to the Devil, for help against the Devil'. It was due to this very act, he warned, that evil had been unleashed, and was directly responsible for the terror that followed. Interestingly, a 17th-century English practice involved feeding cakes made from the suffering person's urine to a dog in order to transfer the sickness from the person to the animal via sympathetic magic, suggesting that this idea was well known on both sides of the Atlantic.

Imps and Demons:
The Witch's Familiar

She came to one Mother Waterhouse her neighbour, a poor woman, when she was going to the oven, and desired her to give her a cake, and she would give her a thing that she should be the better for so long as she lived; and this Mother Waterhouse gave her a cake, whereupon she brought her this cat in her apron and taught her as she was instructed before by her grandmother Eve, telling her that she must call him Satan and give him of her blood, and bread and milk as before.

The examination and confession of certain Witches at Chelmsford, 1566

Who has not seen the popular image of a witch with her animal companion – faithful black cat or mud-coloured toad – sitting watchfully by her side? Although nowadays used merely for illustrative purposes, such creatures were once believed to be the witch's very real demon helper, a dangerous co-conspirator and accomplice in a quest to do harm to those that had wronged her.

Accusations and confessions of owning a familiar spirit, or imp as they were often referred to, were a particular mainstay of English witchcraft trials. Reflecting this, the English 1604 Witchcraft Act made it a crime punishable by death if an individual 'shall use, practise, or exercise any invocation or conjuration of any evil and wicked spirit: or shall consult, covenant with, entertain, employ, feed, or reward any evil and wicked spirit, to or for any intent or purpose'.

Agnes Waterhouse, the first woman to be executed for witchcraft in England in 1566, confessed to owning a cat called Satan that did her bidding and took revenge on her enemies. This was just the beginning: in the plethora of trials in England that followed over the next century and a half, familiars featured heavily and became a major element of confessions and interrogations alike.

Witches were believed to use their familiars for a variety of purposes, most often to do harm to others. Ursula Kemp, from St Osyth, Essex, confessed in 1582 to owning four spirits: two were used for punishing and killing, whereas the other two were for causing bodily harm and illness to people, as well as being used to destroy cattle. The aforementioned Agnes Waterhouse confessed that she sent Satan the cat to kill three hogs owned by a Father Kersye, to drown a cow belonging to Widow Goody, and to kill a man with whom she had a feud by a 'bloody flux'. Agnes also followed the example of her sister, Elizabeth Francis, and used the cat to kill her own husband. Mary and Mother Sutton of Milton Ernest, Bedfordshire, were accused of sending their two demons, Dick and Jude, to kill the son of Master Inger after the boy threw stones at Mother Sutton and repeated gossip about her: he sickened and died five days later.

Familiars, when their appearance was described at all, were most often said to appear in animal form. Cats were the most common guise, with dogs, mice and birds being other popular choices. Joan Wallis from Keyston, Huntingdon, described two familiars that came to her in the shape of dogs with great bristles like hogs' hair on their backs. Gwen ferch Ellis of Conwy, North Wales, was believed to have a familiar that took the form of a giant fly, which on one notable occasion terrified men who came to give her a hard time. Elizabeth Bennett and Alice Hunt from St Osyth in Essex were both said to own ferret familiars, and Bennett also had a black dog and another spirit like a red lion. Other animal familiars named included chickens, moles, rabbits, rats, bees and even snails. Some described their familiars as coming to them in human form, most commonly as a man or as a small boy.

In the same manner as pets or animal companions of the time, English familiars often had names and, as with pets, such names were usually either descriptive or human in nature. Margaret Powell from Stowmarket, Suffolk, had three imps called Bess, Nan and Joan, and Ursula Kemp's imps were named Titty, Jack, Pigin and Tyffin. Anne Palmer of Framlingham, Suffolk, confessed to owning two familiars in the shape of turkey cocks – they were named Great Turkey and Little Turkey. Other names, although strange to us today, actually had meaning that made perfect sense to contemporaries: for instance, in the case of the oft-cited Grizzle Greedigut, 'grizzel' was a term used to describe grey animals, and 'greedigut' simply meant someone who was gluttonous.

The ability of the familiar to change their appearance or form was also frequently reported. Agnes Waterhouse's Satan started off in the form of a cat but, in order to solve the dilemma of his mistress needing to sell the wool he slept on, he helpfully turned into a toad instead. Ann Whittle – alias Chattox of Pendle fame – had a spirit named Fancie that came to her as a spotted bitch, a man and sometimes in the shape of a bear.

Some scholars have highlighted the similarities between belief in familiars and fairy belief in the Early Modern period. Like familiars, fairies were believed to be able to impact human life in many of the same ways: causing ill health, in particular to children or animals, impacting farming and fertility, and helping an individual to gain goods and wealth.

Dr Victoria Carr has made a recent case for the ghost familiar. In such situations, a demon appeared in the likeness of a departed loved one, offering to deliver vengeance upon enemies in exchange for becoming a witch. In one poignant example, in May 1647, Margaret Moore of East Anglia confessed to making a pact with the spirits of her three dead children in return for saving the life of the one that still lived. These ghost familiars subsequently carried out several acts of vengeance in her name, including bewitching to death three bullocks and killing a man.

How did a witch come by their familiar spirit? In a similar fashion to confessions of meeting with the Devil, frequently a suspected witch related how the familiar appeared unexpectedly as they went about their daily activities. Also as with the Devil, this often coincided with a time when the accused found herself in a bad situation, in material want or down in spirits – namely, when most vulnerable to manipulation and being take advantage of. In such accounts, the familiar appeared and offered their aid; some 'witches' accepted readily, while others resisted even when offered their greatest desires, and it was not uncommon to hear how a familiar returned two or three times before finally being accepted. Unsurprisingly, many confessed to being terrified when such a creature came to them.

Some said that their familiars had been passed on to them by another witch, and there were many cases of familiars being inherited: from grandmother to mother down to daughter, or from sister to sister. Joan Potter of Hintlesham in Suffolk had four imps; she passed two on to her granddaughter while keeping the other two to kill fowls. Familiars were also passed between neighbours and friends: Ursula Kemp eventually gave her four imps to Alice Newman.

The familiar did not work for free: food and sustenance was the most frequent reward requested by them, and it was generally understood that in return for their help the witch would keep them fed and warm. Many confessed to feeding these creatures, variously with bread, milk, cheese, oats, cake and water. Many familiars were also partial to a drop or two of blood, sucked from a witch's finger or from a teat or mark concealed somewhere on their body. In 1589, Joan Prentice of Sible Hedingham in Essex allowed her ferret familiar to suck a drop of blood from her forefinger, and Alice Hunt from St Osyth was said to have rewarded her ferret familiar with a drop of blood in return for killing six animals belonging to a man that had upset her. Some familiars drove a harder bargain. In some cases, the familiar asked that the witch renounce her faith in God and also made a bargain where the witch would part with her soul.

The relationship between witch and familiar was not always harmonious; there are several accounts where a familiar was violent towards the witch and there were also many occasions when the familiar made promises that they then failed to keep. Things often turned sour, and many lamented how their familiar had abandoned them when they needed them most – usually after they had been accused of witchcraft. It is clear that in English accounts, the familiar often filled the role taken by the Devil in Scotland and elsewhere in Europe.

Belief in familiars lingered long after the end of the witch-trial period, and there is possible evidence for its continuance into the 20th century. An intriguing account from East Anglia makes reference to a witch discovered feeding her 'niggets' –

described as 'creepy crawly things that witches keep all over them' – with pieces of chopped-up grass.

Familiar-like spirits were also sometimes known in places other than England, but there were often substantial differences. In Scotland, where familiars were mentioned they were more often than not in human form, and usually related to accounts of the Witches' Sabbath. In Finnmark, those who made a pact with the Devil were given a personal demon: these were variously referred to as apostles, 'kampan', a 'dreng' or servant boy, and gods. In 1654, Marette Rasmusdatter from Sunnmøre in Norway confessed that her apostle was called Leur and was always in the likeness of a dog that followed wherever she went. According to Marette, she once rode on the dog with another witch named Sigrje, falling off on the Dafre mountain when she felt dizzy. Similar ideas of personal demon helpers can be found in Sweden and Denmark, and this idea also appeared in 17th-century Massachusetts in the Salem witch trials, where accused witch Tatabe accused Sarah Good of having familiar spirits in the form of a cat, a wolf and a yellow bird that sucked between her fingers. In witch trials throughout central Poland and further east, such creatures were seen as part Christian devil, part Slavic house spirit and part ghosts of unbaptized infants.

Protection and Charms:
How to Foil a Witch

One way to gauge what is important to a society or community is to look at the focus and frequency of the customs and superstitions within it. Not surprisingly, due to the widespread and deep-seated belief in the ability of witches to do great harm, there were many and varied ideas regarding how to protect from bewitchment or how to break a bewitchment once it had taken place.

Iron

The healing and protective properties of metal have long been documented, with iron, copper and silver being popular choices. The most frequently mentioned and powerful of these is said to be iron: in 77 CE, Pliny the Elder wrote of its use in medicine, and it was used to avert sickness well into the 19th century. In addition, iron had strong associations with repelling evil, with a long reputation for warding off witches and dealing with all manner of supernatural beings. Pliny again writes how a circle traced with iron or a three-pointed iron weapon carried three times round an infant and adult would protect them from 'noxious influences'.

Horseshoes have been made from iron since at least Roman times, and have long been considered lucky and possessing of protective powers against witches. According to Reginald Scot's 1584 *The Discoverie of Witchcraft:* 'To prevent and cure all mischiefs wrought by these charms and witchcrafts... nail a horse shoe at the inside of the outmost threshold of your house, and so you shall be sure no witch shall have power to enter.'

A horseshoe nailed either above the door of a house or barn or onto the threshold itself was once a familiar and frequent sight in many areas well into the 19th century. The horseshoe could prevent the witch from being able to hurt those within with her curses, or it could act to keep the witch from bodily entering a dwelling. There was also a belief that if a horseshoe was put up while the witch was inside, she would be unable to leave. The belief in lucky horseshoes still exists today, though in most cases the original intent is long forgotten.

Placing protective items made from iron under the bed where an infant or child slept was another common practice. In Wales, a piece of iron or an iron sword was put under the bed of a woman during childbirth in order to provide protection from witches and fairies. In southeastern Europe, various items of metal – including carding combs, scissors, axes, sieves, sickles, iron rings, tongs and copper pots – were placed near the cradle or hung above the door of a room where mother and child lay. On the Isle of Man, a belief was reported in the mid-20th century that if a stranger visited, then metal tongs should be laid across the cradle just in case that person happened to be a witch.

The iron hearth chain was another item believed to be particularly effective against witches. This chain was of central importance in many countries in southeastern Europe, and it was believed to have close links with ancestor spirits and the general luck of the household. In Herzegovina, turning the chain upside down was believed to prevent witches coming down the chimney, while turning it upside down in Poljica, Dalmatia, along with placing an upside-down broom behind the door, would prevent a suspected witch from leaving once she had entered a house. In other areas of Dalmatia, tying the chain in knots would have the same effect.

Doubly potent against witches were sharp objects made of iron, as they were believed to cause extra harm to the witch by scratching her: due to this, sticking pins into an object was a common method of breaking the power of a witch or revealing her identity. A popular choice was a pig's or bullock's heart, filled with pins and hung in the chimney, with the belief that when the heart dried and the pins dropped out, the power of the witch would be broken. In Dorset, a piece of bacon stuck with pins was said to keep witches from coming down the chimney, and driving a nail through the middle of a witch's footprint was believed to break their spell.

Knives were another popular item of protection. In Hvar and Brač, Croatia, scratching the wall with a knife when a witch was trying to choke you was said to leave scratches on her face so that she wouldn't come for you again. This was only successful, however, if no one apart from the victim and the witch knew about the incident. In Orkney, Scotland, knives were placed in the walls of houses to protect against witches and fairies.

There was a general belief that witches were unable to pass over steel, and that placing steel items in entrances would keep them out. Therefore placing a knife or pair of scissors inside the doorway would stop a suspected witch from visiting, as would burying a metal item under the doorstep or threshold. In Essex in the mid-20th century, it was still popular to keep scissors under the doormat to keep witches away.

Scratch the Witch

A particularly popular method of breaking the power of a witch in England and Scotland was that of scratching the suspect with a sharp object. Present in accounts from the start of the witch-trial period, the practice of scratching or 'scoring above the breath' was one of the most frequently used and also one of the most enduring, with incidences cited as late as the 20th century.

Such scratching would ideally be carried out above nose level – hence above the breath – but it was often broadened into a general belief regarding drawing the blood of a witch from anywhere about their person. Scratching could be carried out by friends or relatives of the bewitched, or often the suffering person themselves was the one to scratch the person suspected of causing their misery. If the bewitched individual recovered soon after the scratching occurred, then it was considered proof that the suspect had been responsible.

Although the term 'scratch' implies a minor inconvenience, in reality being scratched was a deeply distressing experience, and in many instances serious harm was caused. The choice of implement used played a part in determining the extent of the resulting damage: anything from a pin or fingernails to darning needles or even, in one instance, a reaping hook, was considered fair game. When 14-year-old Thomas Darling scratched Alice Gooderidge, it was said that her blood 'came out apace', and the practice could even prove fatal: Margaret Francis of Hockham, Norfolk, was said to be about 80 years old when she was scratched by Joan Harvey, and died soon afterwards. Conversely, a lack of blood once scratched was taken as a sign of guilt: Anne Thorn scratched Jane Wenham hard but, despite this, she didn't bleed, and likewise on an occasion when Alice Samuel was scratched, it was said that only water came out.

In Scotland, along with a needle or pin, the nail from a horseshoe was a popular choice, and tree branches were also known to be used. Often whatever sharp object was to hand dictated the implement used to carry out the deed: in 1845 fisherman William Grant from Portmahomack, Easter Ross, believed the elderly wife of another fisherman had cursed him, causing him to lose his new fishing nets and for his crew to refuse to go to sea while he was under her power. Grant cut her with the knife he was carrying, causing such damage that the wound bled for several hours and had to be tended by the local doctor, after which she was confined to bed for five weeks. Grant was imprisoned for three months.

Such assaults were considered not only acceptable but almost standard procedure, necessary for the well-being of the bewitched victim. When Bridget Fox, wife of the vicar of Ilkeston, Derbyshire, fell ill, Anne Wagg, suspected of being behind the bewitchment, was sent for immediately so that her blood could be drawn.

Despite the popularity of scratching, there were voices of dissent. Among them, William Perkins in his *Discourse of Witchcraft* (1608) argued against the practice as he believed it wasn't conclusive proof and was actually a godless act: if an individual recovered after a suspected witch was scratched he believed it was because the Devil chose to let them go, not because he was driven out, and therefore the scratching served no purpose.

Fire

Fire, well known for its cleansing properties, was another potent protection against witchcraft. A popular practice outlined in the *Malleus Maleficarum* and repeated by others in the years that followed involved burning the intestines of an animal suspected to have been killed by witchcraft. These were dragged along the ground towards the house, through the back entrance and into the kitchen, where they were put over the fire. As they heated, so the witch's own intestines would heat up, causing great agony. Writing in 1612, John Cotta recorded that it was believed that the witch would then be forced to go to the place where the burning was taking place in search of a coal from the fire: taking this was the only way for her to stop her suffering. In the Isle of Man in the early 20th century, it was believed that burning a creature murdered by witchcraft could identify a witch: whoever came first to see the burning carcass was the guilty party.

Another fire-related belief recorded by Cotta was that the burning of the suspected witch's excrement or boiling the urine of the bewitched over a fire would make the witch appear. Heating of a pin-stuffed heart was another similar method: in this instance, when the heart burst, the witch's power would be broken.

In 1599, Anne Kerke of London was said to have tormented a young girl through witchcraft. In order to break the spell, her father was advised to cut some fabric from the suspect's coat and burn it, along with his child's undercloth. The child recovered not long after. If someone was already bewitched, it was believed that stealing a piece of thatch from the suspected witch's roof and then burning it would break the spell.

Trees and Plants

The belief in the healing and protective power of certain plants and trees stretches back into antiquity and beyond. Unsurprisingly therefore, there are many plants that have been considered particularly potent against witches and witchcraft, from being able to break an enchantment to repelling a witch altogether.

In Wales, in order to thwart witches, a bunch of fern would be placed over a horse's ears or collar. Another method of gaining immunity involved a male fern, which should be stripped until there were five finger-like fronds remaining. Smoked over a bonfire, they would turn hard, and the resultant 'lucky hand' provided protection against witchcraft. A belief recorded from the northern counties of England in the 19th century was that witches were repelled by ferns because on cutting a fern root horizontally a 'C' – standing for Christ – could be seen.

Certain nuts were said to offer protection: if two walnuts were placed under a chair, it was believed that if a witch then sat on the chair they would be unable to move. Finding a double nut – one where two nuts grew together in one husk – was considered lucky, as it gave protection against witchcraft, and it was common in Perthshire, Scotland, to carry one in a pocket. This was known as a St John's nut, and it was said that although a witch could not be hurt by lead bullets, being shot by a St John's nut would inflict injury against them.

Garlic has long been known for its ability to ward off the supernatural. In southeastern Europe, it was said that witches were deterred by strong smells and therefore rubbing an individual with garlic was believed to be highly effective against them. In Sarajevo, Bosnia, garlic was rubbed on children's chests and the soles of their feet before going to bed on White

Shrovetide (the Saturday before Ash Wednesday) to keep them safe, and in Herzegovina, before going to bed that same night, everyone would taste some garlic in order to prevent witches from seeking out children and eating them. In Serbia, protection against witches for the year ahead could be achieved by placing a bulb of garlic on the windowsill on the Eve of St Thomas's Day, 19 October.

In Scotland, a small amount of ash sap was fed to newborns as their first drink, in the belief that it would protect the infant from witches for the whole of their life. In the north of England and elsewhere, it was believed that carrying a bunch of ash keys – the young, green, immature seeds of the ash tree – protected against witchcraft.

The mountain ash, or rowan as it is more popularly known, was believed throughout Europe to offer protection against evil and witches in particular. Driving a flock or herd of animals through an arch made of rowan was believed to render the animals immune. It was also believed that if a witch was touched by a stick of rowan they would be immediately dragged into hell by the Devil, and planting a rowan close by a house was believed to protect the family within. In Bradfield, near Sheffield, it was recorded that people nailed rowan sprigs to the vessel in which they leavened their oat-cakes in order to keep witches from spoiling the process.

Thorns could also offer protection, and thorn boughs were often nailed above barn doors in order to keep witches out. Some also believed that hanging hawthorn blossoms in the house would mean that witches would get tangled in them and be unable to escape. In some countries in southeastern Europe, the hawthorn is considered sacred and particularly powerful: in Valjevo, Serbia, it was known as the 'witch thorn', and a stake made of hawthorn was believed to repel both witches and vampires, while cradles made from hawthorn were common

protective measures. Thorns also had negative connotations, however: the hawthorn was considered unlucky by some as it was said that it was from a hawthorn that Jesus's crown of thorns was made, and it was also believed in Serbia that sickness-causing demons could live within the wood of the hawthorn tree.

Bladders and Pins: Witch Bottles

Sympathetic magic – the idea that the witch and her victim were linked and that the witch could in turn be harmed through this connection – was at the centre of one particularly popular form of protection: the witch bottle.

Although practices varied, in essence, a stoneware or glass bottle or jar – representing the bladder of the witch – was filled with the urine of an individual believed to be bewitched. Iron nails, pins or thorns were then added, sometimes accompanied by hair or nail clippings of the victim. The bottle would then be either heated or buried, with the idea that doing so would cause the witch pain and force them to break the spell in order to end their own suffering. Creating a witch bottle could also be used in an attempt to locate or identify a witch; in extreme cases, the death of the witch could be the intended aim.

A witch bottle was a form of counter-witchcraft, and was frequently suggested by a cunning man or woman when their opinion was sought on a suspected bewitchment. Sometimes, a sufferer or a family member would take advice from a friend or neighbour. As with many examples of counter-witchcraft, there were those who objected to such practices, as it was believed that these charms were in fact diabolically inspired and using them was tantamount to the very witchcraft they purported to combat.

Evidence of witch bottles exists from the mid-17th century onwards. The majority of specimens have been found in England, with a handful of examples from the USA. Initially, witch bottles were made from stoneware Bartmann ('bearded man') vessels or 'Bellarmines': squat in appearance with a rounded base or belly, the neck of the bottle was marked with a bearded face mask. From the 18th century onwards, however, there was a wider range of vessels used: glass bottles, wine bottles, and small phials in a variety of shapes and sizes became the norm.

There are various accounts containing instances of 'witch bottles' being used. In 1682 a man named Chamblet from London whose daughter had died of presumed witchcraft and whose wife was still ill took the advice of a doctor who advised him to 'take a quart of his wife's water, the pairings of her nails, some of her hair, and such like, and boil them'. As he did so, he heard the voice of the woman suspected – 60-year-old Jane Kent – outside his door. She screamed, and when he saw her the following day she was very bloated and clearly suffering.

Some later witch bottles included written charms. Examples from the late 19th century include those sold by Frederick Culliford, known as the wise man of Crewkerne, Somerset. These bottles included, along with the usual urine and some thorns, a paper reading: 'As long as this paper remains in this bottle of water of mine, I hope Satan will pour out his wrath upon the person that has been privately injuring me . . . they shall not live for more than 90 days from this day, and no longer; and then go into Hell everlasting.'

Creating a witch bottle was not without its practical dangers, and sometimes the process ended in disaster. In 1804 in Bradford, an iron witch bottle exploded when heated by a cunning man, killing his client.

Although the purpose of such bottles was generally to break the spell of a witch, it is believed that some were buried, in particular under the hearth or threshold of a house, in order to offer general protection from evil-doers. Today, this practice is continued by some modern witches.

The earliest known usage of the term 'witch bottle' actually comes from as late as the 19th century, and is not used in Early Modern sources. Cotton Mather, writing in Salem in the late 17th century, for example, referred to the use of a patient's urine to cure witchcraft as the 'urinary experiment'.

The idea of bottling up urine and causing a suspected witch pain can also be found in the folklore of southeastern Europe in a method of identifying witches from Dalmatia, Croatia. On the Saturday before Ash Wednesday, local youths would take a new, unused drinking gourd and fill it with water. Sealing it, they would then walk it around the village before returning to their starting point. There, they would utter the words: 'The witches round whom we have made a circle tonight shall not be able to urinate till we uncork this gourd.'

It was thought that any witches in the area would be overcome with such extreme pain that they would come running to plead for the gourd to be uncorked in order to relieve the terrible pressure in their bladders.

PART THREE

The Witch Cult and Beyond: The Many Paths of the Witch Today

Over the course of the 20th century and beyond there has been a monumental shift in the image of the witch. Starting in the 1930s and 40s and quickly gaining momentum, several modern Neopagan groups came into existence through which the idea and identity of the witch was largely rehabilitated and reclaimed. Whereas in the past the title of 'witch' was a mark of shame, a dangerous identity foisted upon an individual or group by others, in the wake of this rebirth it became a label many chose for themselves, and one that was borne with pride.

Instrumental in this was the passing of legislation that would make British history. The Fraudulent Mediums Act of 1951 was the first time that the crime of witchcraft – either real or pretended – had been off the statute books since the 16th century. It was in the wake of this new freedom that the seeds of many of the practices and beliefs that make up modern witch belief were sown, nurtured and developed by dedicated and charismatic individuals who left their indelible mark on what we know as witchcraft today.

Wiccans, pagans and Neopagans, modern spiritualists, herbalists and healers, and members of feminist and empowerment movements are just some that might use the name 'witch' today, though by no means everyone from those groups will do so. The reasons people identify as witches are as equally varied, and the word has many meanings and interpretations for different people. The terms eclectic witch, kitchen witch, green witch and crystal witch are but a few of the many different expressions of these varied ideas, beliefs and practices within the diverse and colourful melting pot of modern witchcraft.

Thanks to the ever-advancing capabilities of modern technology, witches are able to communicate, share ideas and evolve their craft in ways that were never possible before. WitchTok – the witchy corner of TikTok – is just one of the many popular ways for witches to interact and gain inspiration. The WitchTok-tagged videos – where witches share videos on all aspects of being a witch, offering tutorials, information and details of their life and practice – have a combined viewing of several billion, a figure that is steadily growing.

As in the past, in the 21st century the witch is still a popular figure in books and stories, theatre and artwork, as well as within the modern medium of film and television. But again there is a noticeable shift – whereas once the witch was a maligned figure, to be feared and hated, recent trends see the witch portrayed in a more positive guise, which many can sympathize, and even identify with, and wish to emulate.

How then did this transformation take place? How did the witch go from someone we fear, our greatest enemy, to someone we identify with and want to be?

Margaret Murray and the Myth of the Witch Cult

Of all the ideas that have influenced the development of modern witchcraft, there is none greater than that of the 'witch cult'. First formulated by German academics in the early 19th century before spreading to both France and England, the basis of this popular theory was simple: the individuals persecuted and executed as witches during the witch trials were actually members of an ancient pagan religion, a fertility cult that had been in existence since antiquity. It was believed that, pushed underground by the advent of Christianity and almost wiped out by the witch hunts of the Early Modern period, surviving members had continued to practise their craft in secret.

Although the idea had taken firm hold within academic circles by the end of the 19th century, it wasn't until Egyptologist-turned-folklorist Margaret Murray developed the theory further that the idea reached an eager and receptive public. In 1921 Murray published her ideas in *The Witch-Cult in Western Europe*, and her views quickly became considered an authority. Unlike previous writers, Murray used details from trial records and court documents to provide evidence to back up her claims. Rather than dismissing the details of confessions outright, Murray rationalized the sensationalism of many trial accounts: she argued that the actions and beliefs of those accused had been misinterpreted and wilfully misconstrued, and that those who confessed did so rather than expose the truth of the old religion.

Murray's influence was cemented further when she was asked to write the *Encyclopedia Britannica* entry for 'Witchcraft'. Published in 1929, it remained the official entry until replaced in 1969, thus bringing the theory to a yet wider audience and, stating her theories as proven fact, the concept of the witch cult passed into popular knowledge, influencing and inspiring the imaginations and beliefs of generations to come. Murray further developed these ideas in her book published in 1933, *The God of the Witches*, where she detailed the idea that the ancient religion had one male god rather than many, naming him as the Horned God.

Today, it is widely accepted among academics that there is no historical evidence to support the witch-cult hypothesis. Despite this, one thing cannot be denied: Murray's writings were instrumental in forming the bedrock of many of the original ideas of modern witchcraft, including the most popular of the Neopagan religions today – Wicca.

Gerald Gardner, forefather of what we now know as Wicca, was greatly inspired by Murray's writings. He subsequently stated that Wicca was the modern survival of the religion she described and, furthermore, it was Murray's descriptions of dancing, feasting, songs and spell casting – based on trial records and documentary evidence – that influenced Gardner when it came to developing the early rituals and liturgy of his own tradition. In general, Murray's ideas have had a great and lasting impact on popular beliefs about witchcraft to this day.

The Advent of Wicca

Wicca is one of the largest and most popular organized expressions of witchcraft belief today, and an officially recognized religion in the USA, UK, Canada and Australia.

Although beliefs and practices differ between traditions and groups, today many Wiccans worship a pair of deities in the form of a goddess and god, along with observing some or all of the seasonal festivals known as the Wheel of the Year. As its basis, Wicca uses a blend of ancient and modern writings and ideas, a rich and nuanced synthesis of the old and the new.

It is important, however, to note that not all Wiccans, nor indeed all Neopagan groups, call themselves witches. Some choose to avoid the word and the negative connotations it can carry. Likewise, although recognized as such, not all use the term 'religion', preferring instead to use 'spiritual path' or 'way of life'.

Within Wicca there are many different groups and offshoots, likened by some to denominations within Christianity and Buddhism. The earliest and one of the most prominent of these came to be known as Gardnerian Wicca, named after its greatest spokesperson, Gerald Gardner. As a group or movement,

Wicca can be traced to the activities and writings of Gardner in England during the 1940s and 50s, and – as mentioned above – he is now widely acknowledged as the 'Father of Wicca'.

Gardner had a keen interest in witchcraft and the occult, which he further developed during his travels in the early decades of the 20th century. According to one version of his story, in 1938 upon moving to Highcliffe, near the New Forest, he happened upon the Rosicrucian Theatre in nearby Christchurch. After joining the company of players there, he was in turn introduced to an individual referred to as 'Old Dorothy', and, according to Gardner, he soon discovered that this new acquaintance was actually the head of the only surviving coven of the Old Religion. He was initiated into the group in 1939, and, for Gardner, the existence of this group was firm proof that the religion described by Murray existed. Gardner later revealed that he believed his grandfather had been a witch before him, and that one of his ancestors had been burned as a witch in the 17th century.

In the 1950s, based on the ideas he learned from this coven, Gardner formed his own group, the Bricket Wood Coven. Central to Gardner's claims was his 'Book of Shadows', which he said had been given to him by the coven and contained writings that had been passed down from one successive generation of witches to the next.

The text was an eclectic mixture of writings, with influences including renaissance texts such as *The Key of Solomon*, writings from spiritualism, theosophy, Freemasonry, Aleister Crowley, Charles Leland and James Frazer, along with Gardner's own ideas. It is now generally believed – a view shared by his eventual High Priestess Doreen Valiente – that Gardner wrote much of the Book of Shadows himself, and doubt has been cast regarding whether the New Forest Coven indeed existed. Regardless of its origins, however, this book – and Gardner's beliefs – formed the building blocks of Wicca as we know it today.

Gardner published two witchcraft-based novels during his life, the second of which, *A Goddess Arrives*, was published in 1949 by the owner of the famed Atlantis Bookshop in London. It is in this book that he first portrayed the old witch religion, albeit in a fictionalized form. In 1954, Gardner published the most influential of his works, *Witchcraft Today*, in which he fully presented the tradition to the world for the first time. Covens were led by a High Priestess, along with the High Priest of her choice, and within the tradition there were three degrees of initiation, with only someone already initiated being able to initiate others into the group. The book also included a variety of rituals, including that of 'Drawing Down the Moon', which is considered an important and powerful ritual by many Wiccans today.

Within Gardner's writings, several ritual tools are mentioned, with the most central of these being the black-handled knife. It is in Gardner's Book of Shadows that it is given for the first time the name it is known by today: the athame. According to Gardner, the athame was 'the true witch's weapon' and it remains the most important ritual tool for many within this tradition and others. For Gardner, and many today, the athame is used to cast a circle, and is linked with fire and the masculine; whereas others see the athame as associated with the element of air instead.

Gardner went on to publish *The Meaning of Witchcraft* in 1959, further developing the ideas in *Witchcraft Today*, and he also authored many articles and essays about witchcraft and the occult.

Despite infighting and other dramas, Gardner's coven continued to grow and other Wiccan groups were established in the years that followed, with the movement greatly gaining in popularity and geographical reach. Gardner initiated many individuals into the tradition during the late 1950s and the

1960s, and it was through this that some of the tradition's most influential and well-known high priestesses entered the movement and were largely instrumental in its spread across the UK. Notable among them were Doreen Valiente; Patricia Crowther, who formed covens in Lancashire and Yorkshire; Lois Bourne, who became High Priestess of the Bricket Wood Coven; and Monique Wilson, who founded two covens in Scotland.

It was in this way that Wicca spread not only throughout the UK, but also to Australia and the United States; it was two of Wilson's initiates – Raymond and Rosemary Buckland – who in turn founded the first recorded Gardnerian coven in the United States in 1963, and brought Gardner's Book of Shadows across the Atlantic. Wicca rapidly proliferated there throughout the 1960s and 70s: it is believed that today there are over 200,000 who identify as Wiccan in the United States alone.

Through his involvement with Cecil Williamson, Gardner became involved with the Folklore Centre of Superstition and Witchcraft on the Isle of Man. The museum was opened by Williamson in 1951, and Gardner and his wife moved to the island in the same year, where he became known as the 'resident witch'. Gardner bought the museum from Williamson in 1954, and continued to run it until his death; the museum itself remained open until 1970.

In 1964 at the age of 79, Gardner died from a heart attack, fittingly, it might seem, while reading a book about magic after breakfast aboard the ship the *Scottish Prince* while returning from wintering in Lebanon. He was buried in Tunis, Tunisia. In England, a blue plaque was donated by the Centre for Pagan Studies in 2014, and can be seen at his house in Highcliffe, Dorset, where he lived during the years 1938–45, naming him as the 'Father of Modern Witchcraft'.

Robert Cochrane and Traditional Witchcraft

Do not do what you desire – do what is necessary.
Take all you are given – give all of yourself.
What I have – I hold!
When all else is lost, and not until then, prepare to die with dignity.

An Old Witch Law according to Robert Cochrane

Concurrent with the time Gardner was developing Wicca, other groups started to emerge that likewise asserted to be direct descendants of the witches of old. Including influential figures such as Sybil Leek, Charles Cardell and Raymond Howard, such groups tended to refer to themselves as practising Traditional or Hereditary Witchcraft, in a deliberate distinction from Gardner's Wicca, claiming older, more traditional, roots, although this cannot be proven one way or the other.

One of the most influential of these strands was that created by Roy Bowers or Robert Cochrane as he came to be known. Known as Cochrane's Craft, Cochrane established himself as being in direct opposition to Gardnerian Wicca, and there was no love lost between the two founders.

After a short-lived first coven in the early 1960s, Cochrane established a second group named the Clan of Tubal Cain after the first blacksmith as mentioned in the Bible, and a potential nod to Cochrane's previous work in that profession. In November 1963 he came to popular attention with an article published in the spiritualist newspaper *Psychic News*, stating that witchcraft was the last surviving ancient mystery religion of Europe and asserting his own credentials as a hereditary witch.

Led by Cochrane himself in the role of Magister, the coven worshipped a Horned God and a Triple Goddess. Like Gardner, Cochrane also believed that there was another, greater, deity, the 'Unknown God' behind all others, the primal, central force of creation. Cochrane's tradition favoured working outdoors; the coven frequently met at Burnham Beeches in Buckinghamshire and sometimes on the South Downs near Brighton.

Cochrane and his fellow witches worked clad in black robes, and there was deep symbolism behind many of the locations chosen for rituals and meetings. The main tools in Cochrane's Craft were a ritual knife or athame, a stone used to sharpen the knife, a cup and a ritual cord worn by members of the coven. The item of key importance, however, was a forked staff known as the stang that was said to represent the Horned God, the Goddess or their child, depending on the position it was placed in during a ritual.

Described as young, handsome, with a fiery temper and magnetic personality, Cochrane was an influential and engaging figure. Those who experienced his rituals and gatherings first-hand related how he was a natural leader, drawing those gathered with him to truly powerful spiritual experiences. Despite their later personal disagreements, Doreen Valiente spoke highly of Cochrane, referring to him as 'perhaps the most powerful and gifted personality to have appeared in modern witchcraft'.

Tragically, Cochrane's time on earth was all too brief. After a period of great personal and professional drama, he was discovered unconscious after having ingested belladonna, hellebore and sedatives on Midsummer Eve 1966. He died nine days later on 3 July at the age of 35.

Despite his short life, Cochrane's influence extended well beyond his death and he has left a considerable legacy. Various forms of working have descended from Cochrane and his ideas, and there are many Traditional or Hereditary Witchcraft groups that can be traced back to his influence, including Joseph Wilson's 1734 tradition of American pagan witchcraft. Cochrane's collected writings and letters published as *The Roebuck in the Thicket: An Anthology of the Robert Cochrane Witchcraft Tradition* and *The Robert Cochrane Letters: An Insight into Modern Traditional Witchcraft* appeared in 2001 and 2002 respectively. Several books on Cochrane and based on his teachings have also been published and have had significant influence on Traditional Witchcraft today.

The Mother of Modern Witchcraft:
Doreen Valiente

An it harm none, do what ye will.

The Wiccan Rede

Another crucially important figure in the forging of modern Wicca was Doreen Valiente, and a meeting with Gerald Gardner in 1952 was set to change the face of the then emerging belief system forever.

With a lifelong fascination for the supernatural and the occult, Valiente was already moving in such circles when she and Gardner were introduced by mutual friends. They immediately hit it off, and she was taken into his confidence regarding his developing ideas. Valiente was soon heavily involved, and after being initiated into the Bricket Wood Coven in 1953, she became a prominent figure within it.

Valiente was particularly influential in the area of liturgy writing; Gardner, quickly recognizing her creative talents, soon entrusted her with the majority of the work in this area. For Valiente, the authenticity of Wicca was crucially important, and she quickly recognized the literary influences used by Gardner, often lifted wholesale or with only scant editing. Worried this would detract from the movement's credibility, she convinced Gardner to remove some of the more questionable sources used within his writings, replacing them with her own. Among other key writings, Valiente is generally credited with being instrumental in the creation of the 'Charge of the Goddess', one of the best known pieces of Wiccan liturgy today.

Differing opinions regarding the direction Wicca was taking, along with Gardner's increasing habit of over-sharing with the press, led to rising tensions within the group. The relationship between Valiente and Gardner became increasingly strained, and she eventually broke with Gardner and left the Bricket Wood Coven with several others.

In the years that followed, Valiente was involved with several other groups, including a short-lived coven started with those who had also left the Bricket Wood group, and Raymond Howard's Coven of Atho. It is believed that the first public record of the now popular form of the Wiccan Rede was by Valiente in a speech in 1964, and she was also a key figure in Cochrane's Clan of Tubal Cain, which she joined after meeting Cochrane in the same year. As with Wicca, she lent her considerable literary talents, and was a significant influence on the rituals and ceremonies of this group and Traditional Witchcraft as a whole. Valiente was also a leading figure in the Witchcraft Research Association, and briefly the Pagan Front – later renamed the Pagan Federation – an organization that advocates today for the rights of members of Neopagan groups and promotes general awareness around Neopagan rights. In the years before her death she was a member of the Silver Malkin coven in Brighton, and patron of the Centre for Pagan Studies. A prolific and skilled writer, Valiente was also a published author in her own right. Her works remain highly popular and influential today, including *Natural Magic* (1975), *Witchcraft for Tomorrow* (1978) and *The Rebirth of Witchcraft* (1989).

Valiente remained a respected, prominent influence in the world of Wicca and Traditional Witchcraft until her death in Brighton on 1 September 1999, and she continues to be a much-loved figure today. In 2011, the Doreen Valiente Foundation was founded in order to preserve her substantial collection of magical artefacts and manuscripts due to their importance from both a historical and an educational perspective; in line with her wishes, the posthumously published collection of her poems, *Charge of the Goddess: The Mother of Modern Witchcraft*, was released in 2014 to great acclaim. Valiente's contribution to the rituals, invocations and general structure of Wicca has had a lasting impact, inspiring many, and she was the first witch in Britain to be commemorated by a blue plaque; donated by the Centre for Pagan Studies, it can be seen at her former home, Tyson Place, Grosvenor Street, Brighton. It was unveiled, fittingly, on the date of the summer solstice in 2013. Other than Gerald Gardner, whose plaque was unveiled the following year, Valiente is the only British witch to date to have her life commemorated in such a way, a fitting testament to the great influence and enduring legacy of the 'Mother of Modern Witchcraft'.

King of the Witches: Alexandrian Wicca

Inspired by Gardner's initial ideas, several new groups developed from the melting pot of beliefs surrounding Wicca during the 1960s. One of the most prominent of these was Alexandrian Wicca. Developed in England by Alex Sanders – the self-styled King of the Witches – and his wife Maxine, it continues to be one of the most popular traditions within Wicca today.

The exact details of Sanders' initiation are shrouded in mystery, and there are several competing versions of events. It is generally assumed, however, that he was initiated into Gardnerian Wicca at some point during the 1960s and then went on to found his own coven a short time later.

Alexandrian Wicca shared a lot of similarities with Gardnerian Wicca, including the need to be initiated by a witch already within the tradition, three levels of initiation, and the worship of God and Goddess. Sanders' approach differed from Gardner's in that both ceremonial magic and Qabalah – an esoteric tradition based on mysticism and the occult – were incorporated into his teachings and rituals, and remain a mainstay of Alexandrian Wicca today.

Controversial and charismatic, Sanders – either purposefully or inadvertently – garnered publicity and media attention for himself and Wicca: this tendency caused friction within his own covens and in the wider movement in general. His inclination towards public rituals caused further dispute, as many within the tradition erred towards secrecy. There were also concerns regarding his commercialization of the craft, charging for public performances and workshops when others believed that the information he was imparting should remain concealed. All these aspects led to various disputes with prominent members of the pagan community.

As High Priestess and co-founder, Maxine Sanders was a prominent figure within the tradition. She was central to the carrying out of rituals and ceremonies, and was instrumental in developing and shaping the Alexandrian tradition as a whole. She was also influential in training and initiating future members, dealing with the media, providing workshops and writing books that brought the tradition to an eager public.

Janet and Stewart Farrar, both hugely influential figures within the Wiccan community, were initially Alexandrian initiates. Alexandrian Wicca has influenced and inspired several groups, including Chthonioi Alexandrian Wicca and the 'Starkindler Line' and Blue Star Wicca. Today Alexandrian Wicca is practised across the world and is particularly popular in the USA, Canada, Brazil, South Africa, Britain, Australia, Spain, Portugal and Ireland.

Dianic Wicca

Of all the deities that are called upon by Neopagans and those practising witchcraft today, the Goddess Diana stands out as being of great importance to many. Several traditions have arisen that focus primarily on Diana: one of the most popular of these was founded by Z. Budapest in the United States on the winter solstice of 1971, and is focused on women's empowerment and experience. It is believed in this tradition that the Goddess contains all living things within her, including all goddesses from all other cultures. Covens in this tradition consist exclusively of women, and women's mysteries, honouring and celebrating women's life cycles, and celebrating the agency of women to control their own destiny are central, with a focus on healing and affirmation away from patriarchal ideas and violence. There is a belief within Dianic Wicca that due to the completeness of the Goddess – and, by extension, those who follow her – that there is no need for a complementary god to be worshipped alongside her, and so Dianic Wicca, unlike most other traditions, honours only goddesses.

Like many other founders within Wiccan traditions, Budapest states she is a hereditary witch and that she learned folk magic from her mother. She was the founder of the Susan B. Anthony Coven No. 1 in 1971, the first women-only coven, and was the founder and director of the Women's Spirituality Forum. Since 1991, Budapest has also been at the centre of organizing bi-annual Goddess Festivals held in the Californian Redwoods.

So who was the Goddess Diana? The Roman goddess Diana – Artemis to the Greeks – is known variously as the goddess of the countryside, crossroads, childbirth and fertility, nature, the moon and the night. Her strongest association however is as goddess of the hunt; as one of the most powerful of the ancient goddesses, Diana was depicted in most Roman works of art with her eponymous bow and quiver full of arrows.

Daughter of the king of the gods Jupiter and his mistress Latona, Diana was a complex figure. Along with Vesta and Minerva, she was one of the few virgin goddesses, seeking and being granted permission from Jupiter never to marry. Diana was sometimes depicted as a triple goddess, along with moon goddesses Selene or Luna, and underworld goddess Hekate. Diana was both virginal and chaste, while fiercely independent; a fierce protector, tied to no man, she was a fitting choice to head the movement amid the upsurge in feminism and the quest for female power in the 1970s.

As evidence of her importance, a major temple to the goddess existed in Ephesus, modern-day Turkey. One of the largest Greek temples ever built, and the first to be made entirely of marble, the temple was approximately 155m (377ft) in length, 55m (180ft) wide, with 127 columns, each 18m (60ft) high. Taking over a century to build, it was named as one of the Seven Wonders of the World by the famed Greek historian Herodotus, along with – among others – the Colossus at Rhodes and the Great Pyramid of Giza. Built in 550 BCE, the original temple was destroyed by fire in an arson attack, in 356 BCE.

Today, Dianic Wicca remains widely popular, particularly in the United States and Canada where there are many groups, covens and solitary practitioners. Dianic Wicca is also popular in the United Kingdom, some other areas of Europe, and Australia.

The Reclaiming Tradition:
Starhawk and *The Spiral Dance*

Combining worship of the Goddess with feminism and political and ecological activism, the Reclaiming Tradition of Wicca is a modern form of feminist witchcraft. It originated in 1979 in the San Francisco Bay Area with Miriam Simos – known most famously as Starhawk – and Diane Baker, who initially set out to provide a six-week series of classes on Goddess spirituality for women. When these proved overwhelmingly popular, more classes were created and developed, and from this starting point the Reclaiming Collective was created, formed of Starhawk, Baker and a series of former graduates and teachers.

From this beginning, the ideas of the tradition were spread in a variety of ways. The classes remained the mainstay of the tradition, plus public rituals celebrating the Sabbaths, annual Witch Camps and a quarterly newsletter. Starhawk's popular and highly influential book, *The Spiral Dance*, was published in 1979; pioneering for its time and hugely influential both then and now, this further helped spread the ideas of the Reclaiming Tradition to a wider audience.

Like Dianic Wicca, Reclaiming has only one deity – the Goddess. It is also noticeable for explicitly labelling itself as witchcraft. Personal spiritual inner well-being is central to the Reclaiming Tradition and the rituals involved reflect this, with the Spiral Dance ritual for which Starhawk's book was named being of central importance. As the name implies, this is an interconnected chain dance, representing how everyone on earth is linked together, and is performed in many different arenas, both in private or during public gatherings such as protests. There is a strong emphasis within the movement on uniting spirit and politics, along with a focus on personal empowerment and commitment to bringing the work of the Goddess into the world.

Today, the Reclaiming Tradition is a thriving international community of many thousands, based on the teachings of the original collective. Hugely popular autonomous Witch Camps, linked to the Reclaiming representative body by a Witch Camp spokescouncil, are held throughout the USA, Canada and Europe.

Solitary Practitioners:
The Way of the Hedge Witch

Within the first covens of modern witches, the craft was generally held to be a secret, initiatory and group experience. However, a shift occurred in the 1960s and, particularly after the death of Gerald Gardner, the way of the witch became increasingly popular and accessible to all. From this development sprang an increasing number of solitary witches – those who, for whatever reason, chose to work alone rather than joining or forming a coven.

Part of the reason for this development was the wealth of books that appeared in the following years; the writings of prominent witches such as Doreen Valiente, Z. Budapest, Starhawk, Janet and Stewart Farrar, along with Gardner himself, provided inspiration to many. In particular, Charles Cardell's publication of sections of Gardner's Book of Shadows shortly after his death, while controversial, meant the material could be utilized by the solitary practitioner, further aided by the full publication of Gardner's book sometime later. Within the coven structure, there were also several who supported the validity of solitary practice: among them, Doreen Valiente was an early advocate for self-initiation, where an individual makes a private profession of their belief and commitment, and some writers produced self-initiation rituals to aid this.

Writer Rae Beth was among the first writers to specifically cater to the solitary witch. Her first book, *Hedge Witch – A Guide to Solitary Witchcraft* published in the UK in 1990, and as *The Wiccan Path: A Guide for the Solitary Practitioner* in the USA, was hugely influential, and the term 'Hedge Witch' is used by many solitary witches today. In Beth's works there is a focus on grounding within the cyclical seasonal celebrations of the land and the moon, along with a general emphasis on nature and spirituality. A prolific and popular writer, she has written several other books for the solitary witch, including *The Hedge Witch's Way: Magical Spirituality for the Lone Spellcaster*, and *Spellcraft for Hedge Witches: A Guide to Healing our Lives*.

Cecil Williamson – founder of the Witchcraft Research Centre and the Museum of Witchcraft – was also in favour of solitary witchcraft. He coined the term 'Wayside Witches' to describe the lone witch, and said that he gathered his knowledge of magic and witchcraft from various such individuals within the West Country, which he used as the basis for own magical practice.

Today there are many books available for the solitary witch, along with a plethora of workshops, seminars and classes available both online and in person, catering for a wide range of tastes and preferences. Being a solitary practitioner doesn't necessarily mean working alone exclusively – some solitary witches choose to join with others at specific times, such as for certain rituals, celebrations or meetings.

Maiden, Mother, Crone:
The Great Goddess

A goddess figure is of great importance to many modern witches today and she is represented and celebrated in a variety of different ways. Within many Neopagan traditions, this goddess is seen as a tripartite/three-fold goddess; three aspects in one being.

Within Wicca, the Great Goddess – sometimes known as the Triple Goddess – is the most central and important deity followed by some Wiccans. A reflection of the cyclical nature of life and the very phases of life itself, in all of her forms the Goddess has close ties to nature and creation, fertility and life. When represented as the Triple Goddess, the deity is said to have three aspects – the Maiden, Mother and Crone – standing for the three 'stages' or seasons that women pass through in their lives. Sometimes each of these stages is linked to a phase of the moon, with the Maiden representing the waxing crescent, the Mother the full moon and the Crone the waning moon. Some Wiccan traditions also look to a fourth aspect of the Goddess. Known as the Wild Woman or Enchantress, this

aspect represents the untamed, primal forces of nature that lie intrinsically within us all.

In Cochrane's Craft and some Traditional Witchcraft groups, the Goddess is known as the White Goddess, inspired by the poetry of Robert Graves. Also viewed as a threefold deity, these aspects are sometimes known as three mothers or sisters, believed by some to have connection to the three Fates. The White Goddess is also said to be the mother of a young horned god, fathered by the Horned God.

According to Robert Graves, Hekate was the original Triple Goddess and a historical basis for modern Goddess worship. He outlined various ways that the Goddess and her three aspects mirrored and stood for the stages of a woman's life, as Maiden/Nymph/Hag, Mother/Bride/Layer-out, as well as the more familiar Maiden/Mother/Crone.

Although by no means universal, some view the Goddess as the embodiment of goddess energy from a myriad of traditions, worshipping her through her divine aspects. Goddesses from many traditions across the world can be invoked, depending on the personal identification with the archetype and the reason for the invocation. Popular choices include Aradia, a lunar goddess from Italian folklore; the Irish goddess Brigid; and the Egyptian Isis.

From Cernunnos to the Green Man:
The Horned God

Within Wicca and some other Neopagan groups, the Horned God is revered by many today, in partnership with the Great Goddess. Often depicted with horns or antlers to highlight his connection to the natural world, the Horned God is the personification of male energy, and the primal energy from within. Closely linked with nature and fertility, the Horned God can also clearly be seen to represent the cycles of life.

In some traditions, the Horned God is said to be born at Yule as the darker half of the year begins; as the year turns he grows to maturity, reaching his peak at midsummer where he dies, only to be reborn again as Yule comes round once more. Some personify the two aspects as the Oak King and the Holly King. These two symbolize the shifting of the seasons as the year rolls onwards, the never-ending battle between light and darkness. The first half of the year, from Yule to midsummer, is the Oak King's domain. His growing power and vitality are reflected in the ever-strengthening power of the sun; reaching the height of his power at the midsummer solstice, he does battle with the

Holly King. The Holly King, always triumphant, reigns over the next half of the year. His domain spans the months until the winter solstice, as the nights lengthen, the days darken and grow colder, and the power of the Oak King is well and truly stamped out. But all is well as, with the winter solstice, the Oak King defeats the Holly King in turn, and so the cycle continues for another year.

As with the Great Goddess, some worship and follow other aspects of the Horned God. Some worship the Green Man, either in his own right, as a symbol of nature, or as an aspect of the Horned God. In some traditions, Wiccans incorporate him into their beliefs and practices, and he is popular throughout many pagan groups. As the name implies, the Green Man is closely associated with nature, and also the cycle of life, death and rebirth. A guardian of the forest, the Green Man is often shown as a face surrounded by greenery such as vines and leaves. A masculine aspect of the Horned God, a symbol of the natural world, the Green Man represents the vitality of the earth.

Another god or aspect sometimes linked to the Horned God is that of Cernunnos. This figure is also depicted as a horned figure, representing his connection with animals and the wild, and he embodies fertility and the abundance of the natural world. Believed by many to have Celtic origins, it is thought that worship of Cernunnos was likely part of ancient religious observance in Europe. Today, either as an aspect of the Horned God or a deity in his own right, Cernunnos is often called upon for guidance, strength and blessings connected to the natural world.

Herne the Hunter is linked with the Horned God by some, an idea popularized in the 1929 *The History of the Devil – The Horned God of the West* by R. Lowe Thompson, where it is suggested that Herne and Cernunnos are one and the same. Herne is a ghostly horned figure most closely associated with the

Windsor Forest area of Berkshire, England, where he was said to ride his horse while rattling chains and terrifying cattle as he went.

In Traditional Witchcraft as put forward by Robert Cochrane, the God is associated with fire, time and the Underworld, and was known variously as Wayland, Herne, Tubal Cain and Bran. According to Stregheria, modern Italian witchcraft, the God is known by several names, including Dianus, Faunus, Actaeon and Cern. Within Wicca, Stewart Farrar named the God Karnayna, whereas Doreen Valiente referred to him as Cernunnos or Janicot, citing the latter from Gardner and speculating that it was potentially the name used by the New Forest Coven. Raymond Howard and Charles Cardell called the God Atho or Athor.

The Wheel of the Year

The concept of the Wheel of the Year is familiar and important to many pagans and those who identify as witches today. The wheel marks the cycle of the sun passing through the sky, the earth rotating around it, the cycle of life, death, rebirth and renewal itself.

The Wheel as it is now known consists of eight festivals known by some as Sabbats. These Sabbats or spokes of the wheel are made up of the natural solar divisions of equinoxes (the point when the sun is directly above the equator) and solstices (when the sun reaches the highest point in the sky at each of the two poles), and the cross-quarter days that fall between them.

Modern witches observe the Sabbats in different ways, marking the passage of time how they see fit. Although observing eight Sabbats is most common, some observe only the four solar festivals, while others may select their own pattern of festivals to follow based on personal preference.

The wheel in its present form is relatively recent, but the fact that these dates have been celebrated in cultures and societies across time and geographical space is testament to the fact they are of great intrinsic importance to our collective human psyche. The observance of many of the festivals included within the wheel has a long history, important to different people at different times; today, many of the current observances are based on and have roots in older, folk traditions and beliefs.

The names used here for each Sabbat are those most commonly used today: there may however be variation between groups or individuals.

Summer's End: Samhain

Better known to many today as Halloween, Samhain – from the Irish 'summer's end' – is believed to have its roots in pre-Christian tradition, and marks the midpoint between the autumnal equinox and winter solstice. Samhain was the last of three agricultural festivals of the pagan year and marks the coming of winter; with Samhain comes the first chill in the air, heralding the shorter days to come. Samhain is a liminal time, a time of transition as the wheel slides from one season to the next. Death, transformation, ancestor worship and remembrance are common themes today at this time.

There is strong evidence that a major festival took place at the start of November across the British Isles in areas where a pastoral economy was present. At Samhain it was believed that both people and spirits could move between the worlds of the living and the dead, and it was also a time of fairies, witches and otherworldly creatures. In the Shetland Isles, the trows – a mischievous fairy-type spirit – were said to cause mischief to both crops and cattle.

Until the early 19th century, a practice known as 'lating' or hindering witches was observed in Lancashire at this time of year. People would walk the hillside of Longridge Fell between 11pm and midnight, with lighted candle in hand. If the candle blew out, then this was a sign that a witch was nearby and that precautions needed to be taken. In many areas, it was also generally advised to avoid churchyards and crossroads at this time owing to a belief with the belief that they would be awash with spirits and bad beings. In southern Ireland, a cross of sticks woven together with straw known as the *parshell* was a popular form of protection. This was placed on the inside of the house, over the entrance, and believed to give protection to those inside.

Fire-related traditions were popular on this date in northern and central Wales, the areas close to the line demarking the Scottish Highlands, and the Isle of Man, though there is no evidence of a widespread Celtic fire festival. The later Christianization and association with the Feast of the Dead/All Saints only further cemented the time as one associated with spirits and the supernatural, and was likewise a time when ancestors were honoured and remembered.

Linked with divination and magic, rituals and rites were often practised on this day. In later times, particularly popular in the 19th century, some of these became the games we now associate with Halloween. Popular rites included the peeling of an apple: by keeping the peel whole and throwing it over one shoulder, the shape it landed in revealed the initial of the person's future spouse. Another common prophetic practice for couples was placing two nuts in the fire – if they stayed together then all would be well, but if the nuts sparked and jumped apart, then the relationship was doomed. As reflected in such practices, those born on Samhain were believed to have divinatory power, bestowed upon them by the nature of that night.

Burning the Yule Log: Yule

The midwinter festival of Yule or the winter solstice falls between 20 and 23 December in the Northern Hemisphere, the shortest day of the year. This time, when night is at its longest and darkest, has been celebrated by countless cultures and societies throughout history, and is perhaps the most widely observed across the world today.

Yule marks a time of feasting and celebration, of much-needed leisure time after the hard work of the harvests. By this point, food was stored away ready for the cold, long winter, with the hope that provisions would last through the dead months ahead. Marking an important turning point in the year, Yule is also a time of relief and rejoicing. From this moment onwards, the days start to lengthen again, imperceptibly at first but with increasing certainty, each new dawn bringing a little more light than the last.

The Holly King, with dominion over the dark half of the year, reaches the peak of his power at Yule. Like the Oak King at midsummer, however, it is at this very moment that he begins to lose his grip on the year, as the wheel turns inexorably on, and suddenly the Oak King is in the ascendant, bringing with him a return of the light. Yule also signifies the rebirth of the Horned God and the return of the life-giving energy of the sun.

One of the most popular and oldest traditions associated with Yule is the custom of the Yule Log, found in the UK, North America and Europe. Simply put, a log was chosen – often the biggest or best-looking for the purpose – taken into the house and burned throughout the midwinter period. There were many beliefs and practices attached to this ritual, varying from area to area. In areas of Scotland and Norfolk, England, among others, good alcohol was only received while the Yule Log burned; a good incentive to find the largest log possible! Many believed it was lucky to keep a piece of the log to light the log of the following year. Another common belief was that keeping the log under the bed could prevent lightning; in Somerset, England, it was believed that doing so could also prevent chilblains.

Greenery and evergreens have a long association with midwinter and Yule. Mistletoe, holly, pine, ivy and oak were popular decorations at this time, and were often believed to be imbued with protective properties. Accordingly, they were placed around windows, doorways and other points of entry. There are several superstitions regarding how long said decorations should remain up and how they should be disposed of: a popular belief was that the Yuletide greenery should be burned in order to avoid bad luck, either by Twelfth Night on 5/6 January, or Candlemas, 2 February.

In the Belly: Imbolc

Imbolc was traditionally observed at the midpoint between the winter solstice and spring equinox. Typically held on 1 or 2 February, this was an important milestone in the yearly cycle, marking the wonder and hope that is associated with the return of the light of spring and of warmer times ahead.

There is much debate regarding the origins of this festival, but it is clear that it was observed in pre-Christian times and was and continues to be of great importance. There is evidence for the significance of this date from the Neolithic period onwards: among others, at the prehistoric passage tomb known as the Mound of the Hostages on the Hill of Tara, County Meath, Ireland, the inner chamber is illuminated by the rising sun at Imbolc. There are also records of a festival at this time in 10th-century Irish sources, although there is no indication of what this originally celebrated or how it was observed.

There are several suggested origins for the name Imbolc. One idea is that it comes from the Old Irish *Imbolg*, meaning 'In the belly', referring to the fact that ewes are pregnant at this time. Another idea is that it comes from an old Irish word for 'cleansing'. The festival is also called *Imbolg* and *Oimlec*.

Imbolc has connections with the Irish St Brigid, whose festival is also observed on 2 February, and it is generally accepted that a pagan goddess of the same name pre-dates the saint. The Goddess may have already been associated with this time of year, which in turn may have influenced the date on which the Christian saint was later venerated. Brigid is another deity associated with the Great Goddess and is sometimes worshipped as an aspect of the Triple Goddess with her connections with healing, the hearth, and the sacred feminine.

St Brigid was particularly revered in Ireland, Scotland and the Isle of Man. In Ireland, St Brigid of Kildare came second only to St Patrick himself, and she was the saint of several things, including healing, poetry, livestock and dairy production, learning and blacksmiths. There are various legends attached to Brigid, including that she was a wet nurse to Christ himself. Snowdrops are often associated with this festival: known as 'Brigid's flowers', they are signs of hope for the ending of winter and the start of spring, symbols of purity and transformation.

In the 19th century, St Brigid celebrations began on the evening of 31 January. St Brigid's crosses were made from rushes, a celebratory meal was held, and images of the saint – *Brídeógs* – were made, along with special beds to receive them. It was believed that Brigid went from house to house, blessing each as she went, and items of clothing or a piece of cloth were often left outside for her to bless. The crosses were seen as symbols of protection, to both people and livestock. Brigid was also closely associated with wells, and many in Ireland bore her name. People would make pilgrimages to them at this time and leave offerings and make prayers and wishes there. Brigid remains an important figure in Imbolc celebrations today.

This time of year is also closely associated with returning light, and Candlemas, celebrating the presentation of Jesus at the Temple, also falls around this time. Candles are also popularly associated with Imbolc and this time in general, likewise symbolizing the light returning to the world.

Much store is held by what the weather is doing on Imbolc, and another figure associated with the time is the Cailleach. This Gaelic divine hag is said to leave her house on this day to gather firewood: if the weather is fine, beware, for the winter is far from over, as the Cailleach gathers plenty of wood to keep her going throughout. If the weather is bad, however, rejoice, for the Cailleach remains asleep, and winter will soon be over for another year.

New Life: Ostara

The festival of Ostara is associated with the first official day of spring, the vernal equinox that, in the Northern Hemisphere, falls at a point between 19 and 22 March each year. On this day, both day and night are the exact same length, the cosmos held in a delicate balance for one fleeting moment before the wheel again turns on its way.

It is said that at Ostara the Maiden Goddess finally awakens from her long sleep of death, and these themes are summed up in the story of Persephone from Ancient Greece. The beautiful young daughter of Zeus and Demeter, the goddess of the harvest, Persephone was abducted one day by Hades, King of the Underworld. Distraught, Demeter searched in vain for her daughter, her grief causing the crops to wither and eternal winter to descend upon the earth. Zeus intervened and demanded the return of the young maiden, but, alas! Persephone had eaten pomegranate seeds during her time in the Underworld, meaning she was inextricably bound to it. A compromise was reached: Persephone would spend half the year with Hades – a month for each seed she had eaten – and half in the world above with her mother. During her daughter's absence, winter falls as Demeter grieves afresh, to be replaced by the flowers and greenery of spring when Persephone returns to her. Accordingly, Ostara is a time for great rejoicing and celebration, focusing on rebirth and new life.

The origins of this festival are largely unknown, and there has been much debate and invention surrounding it. At the centre of this debate is the proposed connection to the goddess Eostre, after whom many believe the festival is named. Although said to have a long history, it is surprising to learn that the only historical mention of Eostre comes from the Venerable Bede in the 8th century, who made the assumption that the old name for April – *Eosturmonata* – was based upon an ancient goddess. This idea was popularized in the 19th century by Jacob Grimm in his 1835 *Deutsche Mythologie.* Taking inspiration from Bede, Grimm decided that the goddess Ostara was a local version of a wider Germanic goddess, and she became a living figure in the popular imagination, although debate continues regarding whether Bede invented or imagined the goddess himself. The modern name of Ostara was given to the festival by Aidan Kelly in the 1970s, in turn using Grimm as inspiration. Instrumental in the development of Wicca in the USA, Kelly was highly influential and largely helped shape the Wheel of the Year as we know it today.

Welcoming the Sun: Beltane

Today, one of the most popular of the yearly festivals is Beltane. Observed on 1 May, this was traditionally an important time in the agricultural calendar, marking the start of summer when cattle were sent out into the summer pastures.

The first written mentions of Beltane are from 10th-century Irish literature, where under Beltane is mentioned 'lucky fire'. According to these sources, cattle would be taken to the Beltane fires and would be driven between them, which was believed to bring protection. In Ireland, it was also known as *Cetshamain* – first of summer – and it has been posited that the name Beltane might have replaced an earlier name for the time, *Cetsoman*. Some believe that the word Beltane comes from links to the northern European god Belenus.

Fire – and all its associations with the sun – played an important part in Beltane celebrations, and there is good evidence that the lighting of fires at Beltane was a widespread practice across Ireland, Scotland, Wales, the Isle of Man and parts of England. The over-riding symbolism of such fires was that of protection: a popular practice was that hearth fires in all houses were put out on the evening of 30 April and relit the following day from the Beltane fires in the belief that the household would be protected for the year ahead.

Many also believed that jumping over or walking through Beltane fires would likewise keep them safe from harm, a belief that continues even today. In 1852 it was recorded that a man would leap backwards and forwards three times through the fire for a successful journey ahead. Girls passed across the fire in the belief that it would ensure they had good husbands, and children were carried to bring them protection for the year ahead. When the fires finally died down, the embers were scattered among the crops to bring protection.

Evidence of the importance of Beltane lingers in place names today in Ireland; many contain the world Bealtaine or Beltany (the anglicized version), illustrating that they had associations with Beltane in times past. That it was a popular time for celebration is clear; in 1571 it was recorded that in Peebles, in the Lowlands of Scotland, the watch was doubled on Beltane Eve and Day in order to control merrymaking.

The popularity of Beltane and the lighting of Beltane fires slowly declined throughout the 19th century. In recent years, however, there has been a revival of this old tradition; today, those wishing to celebrate Beltane can attend the annual Beltane Fire Festival held by the Beltane Fire Society on Calton Hill, Edinburgh; Bealtaine Fire Festival at Uisneach Hill, Rathnew, Ireland; and Butser Ancient Farm, Waterlooville, Hampshire, where, among other things, those gathered can witness the burning of a 12m (40ft) Wickerman.

The Longest Day: Litha

The Sabbat of Litha marks the summer solstice, taking place on 21 or 22 June in the Northern Hemisphere. The longest day of the year, when the sun is furthest from the equator, Litha represents the ultimate triumph of light over darkness, as on this day the sun is at its strongest and in the sky the longest. Today, it is at Litha that the Oak King is said to be at full strength. It is, however, at this time he does battle with the Holly King and, as the wheel starts to turn again, the Holly King is victorious, guiding the year down towards darkness once more.

There is strong evidence that celebrations have taken place at this time across Europe throughout history, and that it was a widely held day of feasting and celebration. Fire, as a symbol of the sun, was a common theme of such festivities: one 4th-century source records the popular practice of rolling a flaming wheel – representing the sun – down a hill into a river, and variations of this are found right up into the 19th century. In the Vale of Glamorgan, Wales, a large cart wheel was completely covered with straw. It was then set alight and set rolling down the hill to cheers and shouting – if the flames were extinguished before it reached the bottom, then it was a warning of a bad harvest to come. If the wheel remained alight, however, then a plentiful harvest should be expected. In Devon, England, if the wheel landed in a stream it was believed the community would have good luck for the year – sticks were used to guide its descent to achieve this.

There is archaeological evidence to suggest that the summer solstice was of importance as far back as the Neolithic period. Many stone monuments are believed to have been built in alignment with the rising sun on the solstice; of these, Stonehenge in Wiltshire, England, is perhaps the most famous. Thousands gather there each year to watch as the sun rises behind the heel stone, the growing rays shining through the centre a glorious, magical sight to witness.

In some parts of Europe, older summer solstice traditions also became amalgamated into the Christian feast of St John. Popular traditions included tar barrels paraded around town, torches swung on chains or poles, and bonfires lit on nearby hills. The light of the sun – represented by these fires – was believed to keep evil at bay. The lighting of fires was also seen to increase the strength of the sun, vitally important for the growing of crops and a plentiful harvest.

Start of the Harvest: Lughnasadh

Lughnasadh, celebrated on August Eve, 1 August, marks the first harvest festival of the Wheel, the midpoint between the longest day of the year and the autumn equinox. Historically, this date was important across the British Isles as it marked the start of the harvest season, and it is the first harvest festival of the pagan year.

Lughnasadh – or Lugnasa or Lughnasa – is mentioned in Irish literature of the 11th century and is said to be named after the Celtic god Lugh, who some believe to have been a god of sun and light. Legend says that he created the festival in honour of his foster mother Tailtiu, a mortal woman who died clearing Ireland of woodland so that the ground could be used for growing grain. She perished from exhaustion at the monumental task, and Lugh decreed that a festival be held each year in her honour. It has been suggested, however, that Lugh was not a sun or harvest god at all, and was actually god of general human skills. Interestingly, Lughnasadh is the only major Irish feast to be named after a known deity.

Although evidence that the same festival was celebrated across the British Isles on this date is inconclusive, it is clear that it was a significant time of year. In Ireland, focus was placed on the first harvests that took place around this time, with hilltop gatherings to celebrate the start of the potato and cereal harvests recorded across the 18th and 19th centuries. Likewise, on the Isle of Man at *Laa'l Lhuanys*, there is a long tradition of hilltop worship and celebration. It was customary to gather on hills such as Snaefell and South Barrule, and such gatherings still take place today.

In Scotland, *La-Feill Maire* took place on 15 August, a date that would have been closer to 1 August if not for the calendar change in 1752. People rose early to pick the first of newly ripened corn and make it into *Moilean Maire*, the 'fatling of Mary' bannock, to celebrate the Assumption of the Virgin Mary. Finally, in England, 1 August was celebrated as the festival of Lammas, the old Saxon Hlaf Mass or Loaf Mass, reflecting again the importance of grain and bread at this time.

An old tradition during the Anglo-Saxon period was that the first bread made from the first newly harvested corn would be broken into four pieces. A piece was then set in the corners of a barn where the grain was stored, believed to bring protection from harm and the assurance of plentiful future harvests.

Lammas fairs were popular across the British Isles at this time of year; Ireland's oldest Lammas fair is the annual Ould Lammas Fair at Ballycastle, Northern Ireland.

Gerald Gardner and Operation Cone of Power

Late at night on 1 August 1940, Lammas Eve, it is said that a group of witches gathered in a forest near Highcliffe-by-the-Sea in Dorset. This was no social gathering, however, and the meeting was for a purpose of utmost importance: an attempt to keep Nazi forces from invading England. According to Gerald Gardner, the witches – Gardner among them – raised a Cone of Power, during which they directed a message including the words 'You cannot cross the sea' directly into Adolf Hitler's mind.

The idea behind a Cone of Power is a simple yet effective one; a group gathers and forms a circle, making the base of the cone. Through singing and chanting the same phrases or words over and over, power steadily mounts, until it is released all at the same moment towards the intended target.

Details of this particular mission are shrouded in mystery. Gardner himself didn't claim the ritual had been successful, and there are some that doubt whether the event even occurred at all; Gardner's accounts of what happened are the only contemporary source for what was said to have taken place, and no other attendees have come forward to offer corroboration of his version of events. It has in fact been suggested that the whole idea may have been a clever strategic ploy by Gardner to highlight the patriotism of modern witches at a time when they were being linked with sensational stories of Satan worship and black magic, despite neither ever being part of Wiccan belief. One thing is irrefutable, however: Nazi forces never made it to English shores.

According to Gardner, Operation Cone of Power had a good precedent: he believed that English witches had gathered twice before to see off invasion threats, in 1588 when the Spanish Armada was thwarted, and again in 1805 to stop Napoleon from invading England. Similar group efforts have also taken place in modern times – at the stroke of midnight on 24 February 2017 thousands of witches across the United States took part in a ritual against then President Donald Trump, in the hope of binding him against harmful actions.

Amado Crowley, the self-styled illegitimate son of Aleister Crowley, put forward a conflicting account of events, claiming that Gardner's account was a false creation based on a real ritual that his father Aleister had performed: Operation Mistletoe. According to Amado, who named himself as a witness to events, the ritual took place in Ashdown Forest, Sussex, at the request of none other than MI5. Due to the fact that there is no trace of this event however – or Amado for that matter – in Crowley's extensively detailed diaries or papers for the period, it is likely that this account was influenced by Gardner's Cone of Power account, rather than vice versa.

Harvest Home: Mabon

The festival known as Mabon marks the autumnal equinox, which falls between 22 and 24 September in the Northern Hemisphere, and is celebrated on 20 March in the Southern Hemisphere. At this point, with day and night of equal length, comes the tipping point as the year passes from summer into winter. With Mabon, the night slowly but inexorably wins out over day, a time of gradual change as the year shifts towards its end. The second harvest festival in the wheel, amid the lessening daylight, Mabon marks a time to store food away for the winter ahead.

The autumnal equinox has historically been a time of thanksgiving for the fruits of the earth. Known variously as Harvest Home, the Feast of the Ingathering, *Meán Fómhair*, *An Clabhsúr* or, in neo-druidry, *Alban Elfed*, celebrating a harvest festival around the time of the equinox is common in many cultures, a time of thanksgiving for crops safely gathered and a – hopefully – plentiful harvest. Thanksgiving in America was originally celebrated at the start of October, much closer to Mabon than its current date of 28 November.

Mabon was named by Aidan Kelly in the 1970s; he took inspiration from the myth of Persephone and found a very loose analogy to her story in the Welsh myth of Mabon ap Modron, where Mabon was stolen from his mother and imprisoned in an underwater dungeon. Kelly fixed upon Mabon as the name for this festival and that is how it is widely known today.

Important also at this time is the harvest moon, the name given to the full moon closest to the autumnal equinox. This moon is often witnessed as a magnificent red or orange glowing orb shortly after it rises above the horizon.

A Dark Heritage:
Remembering Our Witches

In the hope of an end to persecution and intolerance.

Memorial to the Bideford Witches – Rougemont Castle, Exeter, Devon

Our journey is almost at its end. But one more issue needs to be highlighted before we go our separate ways. The witch has had a chequered history, and humankind has committed terrible, unimaginable acts in the name of stamping witchcraft out. But what are we to do with this unwanted legacy and how do we address the terrible deeds of the past?

Such questions have long vexed humankind, and opinion has, and continues to be, divided. Some insist that the past should be left in the past, the witch trials and those involved best quietly forgotten. For others it is equally important that we remember what occurred, regardless of the difficult questions and emotions this may raise. This in itself raises a fresh set of issues: if we are to commemorate the victims of witchcraft persecution, what is the best way to go about it?

Salem was one of the first places to commemorate its victims. The first to be remembered was 71-year-old Rebecca Nurse, executed on 19 July 1692 at the height of the Salem witch panic. A monument was erected in 1885 at the Nurse family homestead in the form of a granite obelisk with these words from the poem 'Christian Martyr' by John Greenleaf Whittier:

O Christian Martyr who for Truth could die
When all about thee owned the hideous lie!
The world redeemed from Superstition's sway
Is breathing freer for thy sake today.

Rebecca Nurse, Yarmouth, England 1621. Salem, Mass., 1692.

In more recent times, as the 300-year anniversary of the trials dawned, a public competition was held to design a memorial to mark the event: out of 246 entrants, a design by Maggie Smith and James Cutler was chosen and the finished monument was dedicated on 5 August 1992. The memorial itself is made up of granite walls on three sides, 1.2m (4ft) high: from these at intervals jut 20 simple stone benches, each bearing the name, method and date of execution of one of the victims. Engraved into the stone threshold are words spoken by the victims themselves; taken from court transcripts, these protestations of innocence are chillingly cut short, symbolizing the abrupt ending of the lives of those they commemorate.

Across England, there are memorials of varying sizes to the victims of several of the larger trials that took place there.

As a county, Essex had the highest death toll during the witch trials. In December 2022 a memorial tree was planted in Admirals Park, Chelmsford, along with an information board to commemorate those who lost their lives at nearby South Primrose Hill – over 100 people were executed there for witchcraft during the 16th and 17th centuries. Likewise in Essex, at Colchester Castle, used as a prison to hold over 200 'witches' detected by Matthew Hopkins, there is a plaque commemorating the victims of the Essex Witch Hunts.

On the wall of Rougemont Castle, Exeter, Devon, there is a plaque to commemorate those known as the Bideford Witches or the Devon Witches – Temperance Lloyd, Susannah Edwards and Mary Trembles – the last substantiated individuals to be executed for witchcraft in England in 1682, along with Alice Molland, an accused witch who is believed to have died in 1685. The Bideford Witches were tried at the castle and hanged nearby in Heavitree.

In Scotland, where the death toll was substantially higher, there are many memorials to those who lost their lives. The Witches' Well on Castle Esplanade, Edinburgh, is a cast-iron fountain to honour the hundreds who were burned there during the 16th century – more than at any other single site in Scotland. The Culross Plaque, Fife, commemorates an estimated 380 people who were accused in that area. Lilias Adie, who died awaiting trial in 1704, is remembered in a plaque in Valleyfield, Fife, and also at Torryburn, overlooking the beach where her body was buried in the mudflats, a large sandstone slab placed over her so she couldn't come back to haunt those who had condemned her.

One of the largest monuments to witch-trial victims is the Steilneset Memorial in Vardø, Finnmark, Norway, commemorating the 91 people who were tried and executed there between 1600 and 1692. The memorial was opened in

2011 and consists of two separate buildings. The first, designed by architect Peter Zumthor, is a long wooden structure 125m (410ft) in length: inside there is a fabric cocoon houses a 1.5m (5ft) wide timber walkway, along which there are 91 small windows with a light bulb and accompanying text, each representing an individual who was executed and telling their story. The second building is also by Zumthor, square and made from steel and smoked glass. Inside is an installation by artist Louise Bourgeois named 'The Damned, The Possessed and The Beloved'. This consists of a single steel chair, with flames burning on the seat. The chair is surrounded by a ring of seven oval-shaped mirrors, said to represent judges circling the condemned.

There are several witch memorials where the events they are said to commemorate are debatable or disproven. In Spott, East Lothian, for many years a plaque on the Witches' Stone stated that 'Marion Lillie, the Ringwoodie Witch was burnt here in 1698', said to be the last witch-burning in Scotland. However, records show that although Lillie complained against being slandered as a witch in 1702, she died a natural death three years later and was buried in the Spott kirkyard.

Another memorial to a non-witch is the Maggie Wall monument in Dunning, Perth. The 6m (20ft) high structure consists of a mound of stones with a cross on top and the words 'Maggie Wall Burnt Here 1657 as a Witch'. Legends suggest that Maggie Wall was a maid who had a tryst with the son of a local laird or even the laird himself, while another version has her as a local healer who was persecuted as a witch. The structure appears to only date back to the mid-19th century, however, and theories for the monument's true purpose range from an 18th-century folly, a clearance cairn, or the name of local field Maggie or Muggie Walls. It is also possible that the monument was erected symbolically in memory of all witches, rather than to a particular individual.

These are but a few of the memorials commemorating the victims of the witch trials. First and foremost, they are a reminder of those who lost their lives, ensuring that their names – and what they endured – will never be forgotten. They are also a reminder, stark and unavoidable, of what humankind is capable of doing to its own.

On a more personal level, for descendants of those who lost their lives due to accusations of witchcraft, memorials can serve as closure, a sign of justice in their ancestor's name. They can also provide a place of pilgrimage, a tangible way to connect with their heritage; for example, it is estimated that in the United States, 15 million people are genetically linked to the victims of the Salem trials. Modern witches and practitioners also visit such memorials, both as a sign of respect and as a way of connecting with those they see as linked across time – the witches of old and the witches of the present.

Another, somewhat more contentious, topic surrounding the legacy of the witch trials is the issue of apologies and pardons, and whether these should be granted posthumously to those convicted of witchcraft. A recent upsurge in pardons and campaigns can be seen as part of a wider movement to engage with and make reparation for the past, such as the pardoning in 2006 of 306 soldiers executed for cowardice during the First World War, and more recent apologies made for historical engagement in the slave trade; there is an argument that our witches deserve similar treatment.

As early as 1711, the Massachusetts General Court passed a resolution officially acknowledging the wrongfulness of the convictions and executions that took place in Salem, naming George Burroughs and several other individuals in: 'An Act and Resolve for the Reversing of the Attainders of George Burroughs and Others, For Witchcraft, By the General Court of the Colony of the Massachusetts Bay, in New-England'. In 1957, a resolution was passed formally exonerating all victims of the Salem Trials, stating that they were 'innocent of all crime'. It wasn't until 1992, however, that a bill was finally issued where all of those executed were fully named, and it was later still on 31 October 2001 that they were finally proclaimed innocent.

The guilty verdict against one final Salem witch, however, still stood: 22-year-old Elizabeth Johnson Jr was sentenced to death in 1693, but was reprieved thanks to the collapse that year of the Salem trials. Never formally named on any of the bills that followed, however, she was overlooked and so technically still guilty. Johnson finally found justice over 300 years later, when her case was taken up by an eighth-grade civics teacher from North Andover Middle School in Massachusetts, who used the petition process as a learning opportunity for her students. Thanks to the dedication of Carrie LaPierre and her class, Johnson was pardoned in 2022.

In Europe, on 13 June 1782, Anna Goldi of Glarus, Switzerland, had the dubious honour of being the last person to be executed for witchcraft in Europe. She was also the first to be fully rehabilitated in Switzerland, and in 2008 she was granted a full pardon by the canton of Glarus. Today, a flame burns eternally in the court where she was condemned to death, and there is also a museum in her name, not only to commemorate Goldi, but also to draw attention to human rights and injustices in general today.

Although other pardons occurred sporadically, pardons and campaigns for pardons have noticeably snowballed over recent years, with varying degrees of success. On 31 October, 2004, 81 victims of the Scottish witch hunts were declared innocent. The pardons were granted by the then Baron of Prestonpans, East Lothian, Gordon Prestoungrange. Perhaps uniquely, one of the conditions of the pardon was that the event is commemorated annually with a public ceremony in honour of those accused and executed, with events to be re-enacted every Halloween as a living reminder of the travesty. It was also stipulated that murals should be created depicting the plight of the accused. As a further poignant touch, the baron also pardoned the cats that had been burned alive along with their owners.

Across Germany, the tireless campaigning of Hartmut Hegeler, a retired pastor and religious education teacher, has led to apologies from more than 50 German towns, and Hegeler has also been instrumental in the establishment of plaques and memorials in many areas commemorating witch trial victims. Other momentous developments include the pardoning in 2012 by the Cologne City Council of 38 witches after a unanimous vote in favour and the Connecticut Witch Trial Exoneration Project, created in 2007, that successfully campaigned for the pardoning of 11 people wrongfully executed and over 40 wrongfully indicted in that state. In Spain, in January 2022, the parliament of Catalonia formally pardoned over a thousand individuals – mostly women – executed on charges of witchcraft, and became the first territory in Spain to pass a blanket pardon for all convicted of witchcraft there.

However, not all calls for pardon have been successful. In 1998 a campaign was made for the pardoning of the Pendle Witches. The home secretary at the time opposed the proposal on the grounds that those executed had been convicted according to the laws of the time and therefore a pardon would only be relevant if the original verdict could be proven to be incorrect. More recently, the cause has been taken up again; as of January 2024, a petition for their pardoning reached 10,000 signatures and, at the time of writing, campaigners are awaiting a response from the government.

Dubbed England's 'last witch', Helen Duncan was the last person to be convicted and imprisoned under the 1735 Witchcraft Act. In 1944, she was arrested and, upon trial at the Old Bailey, was found guilty and jailed for nine months in Holloway Prison. Duncan had revealed information regarding a ship that had sunk before this became public knowledge, and it was believed that she was arrested due to concerns of her being a security threat ahead of D-Day. Duncan died in 1956, but in 2007, her granddaughter – who recalled all too well being teased in the playground in the 1940s for being the 'spawn of a witch' – petitioned for a posthumous pardon for Duncan, after a previous attempt in 1999 had been unsuccessful. This attempt likewise failed, as did further campaigns in 2012 and 2016, and at this current time, the verdict against Duncan remains unturned.

In Scotland in 2022, a social media campaign for an apology, legal pardon and national monument for the approximately three thousand people indicted for witchcraft between 1563 and 1736 was launched by the groups Remembering the Accused Witches of Scotland (RAWS) and Witches of Scotland. On International Women's Day 2022, then-First Minister Nicola Sturgeon apologized at Holyrood to 'all those who were accused, convicted, vilified or executed under the Witchcraft Act of 1563' and in the same year a private member's bill was introduced by SNP MSP Natalie Don, proposing the pardoning of all those convicted under the Act. The bill was withdrawn when Don became a minister, however, due to it not being policy for ministers to promote member's bills. Witches of Scotland are currently looking for another MSP to take up the cause.

Obviously, it is too late to right the wrongs of the past and restore the lives that were so unjustly cut short. Some argue using time and energy in the name of those long dead is futile when there are people alive today to be helped instead. It is also suggested that although focusing on such campaigns is a convenient way for people to feel good about themselves and assuage their consciences, little good is actually being achieved.

Then there are those voices – thankfully few in number – who argue that because the individuals involved were convicted under the laws of the time, the sentences should therefore stand. Some go even further and state that those executed had actually been guilty of the crimes they were accused of and, because they believed that they were carrying out witchcraft, their punishment was deserved and just.

Another more nuanced point is whether in the issuing of pardons we are reclaiming and rewriting the past in order to legitimize present grievances. Recent comparisons made between the witch hunts and other acts of genocide, including the Holocaust, for example, are deeply problematic. Official narratives – however well meaning – can also influence outcomes and repaint the past to conveniently fit the present.

For many, however, pardons play an important role, as a symbolic recognition of the victims and the atrocities carried out against them. Pardons and apologies also act as closure for families who, even after many years, feel events as a taint on the memory of their ancestors. It is also argued that obtaining justice serves as a sign to those without a voice today, sending a clear message that injustice, in all forms, will no longer be tolerated. Another basic argument in favour of pardons is the fact that in many cases those accused were convicted on evidence that even at the time was often considered shoddy, much less being able to stand up in any courtroom today.

Witch history has been a great boon to the tourist industry; over two million people are said to visit Salem annually, the vast majority due to interest in the witch trials, while the Museo de las Brujas (the Witch Museum in Zugarramurdi, Spain) and the Anna Goldi Museum in Switzerland draw in thousands of visitors each year. While it is important to remember our witches, there is also the danger that events may be trivialized and neatly repackaged so as not to be offensive to our modern-day sensibilities, and we have a responsibility to ensure that history is preserved and portrayed as authentically as possible. Likewise, tourism brings with it fresh issues; while some leave offerings and notes at such memorials, others come in the hope of gaining a souvenir. The Salem monument, for instance, has been at risk of disrepair due to the number of people taking away pieces of stone as mementos.

Over the last hundred years, the negative connotations associated with witches have been challenged, and the identity that was once so unwanted has been reclaimed and owned as one of independence and strength. In more recent times, the impact of this shift can be seen in very real changes such as increased recognition within the military and the introduction of pagan chaplains in hospital and prison settings. This move is also reflected in our popular media such as books, films and artwork – through the likes of *Buffy the Vampire Slayer*, *Sabrina the Teenage Witch* and *Frozen*'s Elsa, to name but a few, audiences have been introduced to a more likeable, sympathetic witch, and fictional witches are now more often role models rather than predators to be feared. Despite such shifts, however, the change is far from wholesale: many modern witches across Europe and the USA still receive harsh judgement and negativity, along with experiencing physical and verbal attacks for their beliefs.

Globally, the picture is also far from bright. The stark fact is that witchcraft and being labelled as a witch is still a crime punishable by death in some areas of the world, and even if it is not legally an offence, in many areas those accused of being a witch still face torture, torment and death. Worldwide, cases of witchcraft-related violence have actually been on the increase over the last few decades. It is estimated that in Tanzania, East Africa, between 1960 and 2000 approximately 40,000 people accused of witchcraft were murdered. In India, since 2000, over 2,500 women have been killed, with over 1,500 of those taking place between 2010 and 2021: despite legislation against such persecution, accused witches face being burned, lynched, beaten, paraded naked through the streets or having their nails ripped out.

In a disturbing trend caused by increasing levels of urban poverty, growing numbers of accusations of witchcraft against children have been identified across Africa in recent decades. In the Democratic Republic of the Congo alone there are thousands of 'children of witchcraft': blamed for issues such as illness within the family or for being born out of wedlock, they are accused of witchcraft and left to fend for themselves on the streets. In 2024, in Angola, southern Africa, it was reported that around 50 people died after being forced to drink a herbal concoction in order to prove that they were not witches.

While organizations and governments are working together to find effective solutions, the end is far from in sight, as those branded as witches are attacked and ostracized, living in fear for their lives. While it may be comforting to our modern sensibilities to condemn such beliefs and actions as caused by perceived superstition, to do so is both erroneous and dangerously simplistic, a gross failure to understand and identify that such situations are, in reality, much more nuanced.

Finally, it is vital that if we remember one thing only, it is this: the history of the witch is not something neat and tidy that can be compartmentalized and relegated to the past. It is brutal and bloody, filled with pain and injustice, and, while we have come far, the journey is far from over: as long as individuals are ostracized on the basis of being different from ourselves, the spectre of the witch's dark history will remain with us.

Acknowledgements

Adding the finishing touches to a book is always a poignant moment and it is particularly so in this case, being almost a decade ago that I started to write my first book about witches. There is now just one more important task to do: acknowledging some of the very special people who have been with me for the journey of writing *The Story of Witches*.

A heartfelt thank you as always goes to Dee Dee Chainey for her ongoing friendship, support and professional feedback on various drafts throughout the writing process. It is a rare and wonderful thing to find in someone that perfect blend of friend and co-worker, and as an added bonus she has yet to disown me over my overenthusiastic use of commas and rogue capitalization. Thank you!

Huge thanks likewise to Mark Norman for feedback, editing suggestions and general moral support throughout the last, somewhat turbulent, weeks before submitting this manuscript. Thanks also for the sneak peek at his wonderful chapter on witches in *Scooby Doo* from the even more fabulous *Zoinks! The Spooky Folklore behind Scooby Doo* – go order it now so you can read it for yourselves.

Thank you also to Dr Katy Soar for casting her expert eye over the Hekate section in the name of making sure I didn't completely make a mess of it all. Any mistakes that remain, however, are all my own.

Also, a massive thanks to everyone at Batsford Books for all the hard work involved behind the scenes in making this book a reality, and for providing the opportunity to write about a subject so close to my heart.

My children: as always, for their unconditional love, and for simply being themselves. Likewise for such thought-provoking questions as 'What's for tea?' 'Can we watch *Neighbours* yet?' and 'Do chickens have nipples?'

Our cats, Hector and Jayfeather, for providing much-needed distraction and entertainment during the inevitable ups and downs of the writing process. For the record, however, sitting on my laptop still does not count as helping, no matter how cute you look.

To the makers of mini eggs everywhere – this book could not have been written without you. I thank you, even if my bank balance does not.

My main thanks, however, go to you, the reader – thank you, for picking up this book. If it has been an interesting and thought-provoking read then I have achieved what I set out to do and can rest happy. Please do let me know what you think of it; I would love to hear from you, either on X @WillowWinsham or via my website (willowwinsham.com).

And finally, it is time to take a moment to acknowledge witches everywhere – for without them, this book would have been neither necessary nor possible.

Select Bibliography

The following resources may provide useful extra information for readers who want to learn more.

Bek-Pedersen, K., 'Macbeth and "The Weird Sisters" – on Fates and Witches', *Scottish Studies*, vol. 39, 2022, pp. 58–80

Breslaw, Elaine G., *Tituba, Reluctant Witch of Salem*, New York, New York University Press, 1997

Briggs, Robin, *Witches and Neighbours: The Social and Cultural Context of European Witchcraft*, Penguin, 1996

Carr, Victoria, 'Witches and the Dead: The Case for the English Ghost Familiar', *Folklore*, vol. 130, no. 3, 2019, pp. 282–99

Cornish, Helen, 'Cunning Histories: Privileging Narratives in the Present', *History and Anthropology*, vol. 16, no. 3, September 2005, pp. 363–76

Cornish, Helen, 'Spelling Out History: Transforming

Witchcraft Past and Present', *The Pomegranate*, 11.1, 2009, pp. 14–28

Cotta, John, *A Short Discoverie of the Unobserved Dangers*, London, 1612

Davidson, L.S., Ward, J.O., *The Sorcery Trial of Alice Kyteler*, North Carolina, Pegasus Press, 2004

Davies, Owen, *Popular Magic: Cunning Folk in English History*, London, Continuum, 2007

Davies, Owen, *Witchcraft, Magic and Culture 1736–1951*, Manchester, Manchester University Press, 1999

Ewen, C. L'Estrange, *Witch Hunting and Witch Trials*, London, Kegan Paul, Trench, Trubener & Co., 1929

Ewen, C. L'Estrange, *Witchcraft and Demonism*, London, Heath Cranton, 1933

Gardner, Gerald B., *Witchcraft Today*, New York, Magickal Child, 1982

Gaskill, Malcolm, *Witchfinders: A Seventeenth-Century English Tragedy*, London, John Murray, 2005

Gibson, Marion, *Early Modern Witches: Witchcraft Cases in Contemporary Writing*, London, Routledge, 2000

Gibson, Marion (ed.), *Witchcraft and Society in England and America, 1550–1750*, New York, Cornell University Press, 2003

Gibson, Marion, *Witchcraft: A History in 13 Trials*, London, Simon and Schuster, 2023

Heselton, Philip, *Doreen Valiente: Witch*, The Centre For Pagan Studies, 2016

Heselton, Philip, *Gerald Gardner and the Cauldron of Inspiration*, Somerset, Capall Ban Publishing, 2003

Hoggard, Brian, *Magical House Protection: The Archaeology of Counter-Witchcraft*, Berghann Books, 2019

Howard, Michael, *Modern Wicca: A History from Gerald Gardner to the Present*, Llewellyn Publications, 2010

Hutchinson, Francis, *An Historical Essay Concerning Witchcraft*, London, 1718

Hutton, Ronald, *The Triumph of the Moon: A History of Modern Pagan Witchcraft*, Oxford, Oxford University Press, 1999

Karlsen, Carol F., *The Devil in the Shape of a Woman*, New York, Norton and Company, 1998

Kvideland, Reimund, and Sehmsdorf, Henning K., (eds.), *Scandinavian Folk Belief and Legend*, University of Minnesota, Minneapolis, 1988

Levack, Brian P. (ed.), *The Oxford Handbook of Witchcraft in Early Modern Europe and Colonial America*, Oxford, Oxford University Press, 2013

Lowensteyn, Machteld, 'Unravelling the Myth and Histories of the Weighing Test at Oudewater: The Case of Leentje Willems', *Cultures of Witchcraft in Europe from the Middle Ages to the Present*, Barry, J. et al (eds.), Palgrave Historical Studies in Witchcraft and Magic, 2018, pp. 101–20

Macfarlane, Alan, *Witchcraft in Tudor and Stuart England*, London, Routledge, 1999

Mackay, Christopher S., *The Hammer of Witches: A Complete Translation of the Malleus Maleficarum,* Cambridge, Cambridge University Press, 2009

Merrifield, Ralph, 'Witch Bottles and Magical Jugs', *Folklore*, vol. 66, no. 1, 1955, pp. 195–207

Motz, Lotte, 'The Winter Goddess: Percht, Holda, and Related Figures', *Folklore*, vol. 95, no. 2, 1984, pp. 151–66

Murray, Margaret, *The Witch Cult in Western Europe*, London, Oxford University Press, 1921

Nildin-Wall, Bodil, and Wall, Jan, 'The Witch as Hare or the Witch's Hare: Popular Legends and Beliefs in Nordic Tradition', *Folklore,* vol. 104, no. 1–2, 1993, pp. 67–76

Opie, Iona, and Tatem, Moira, (eds.), *A Dictionary of Superstitions*, New York, Oxford University Press, 1989

Ostling, Michael, 'Babyfat and belladonna witches' ointment and the contestation of reality', *Magic, Ritual, and Witchcraft,* vol. 11, no. 1, 2016, pp. 30–72

Paterson, Laura, 'The Witches' Sabbath in Scotland', *Society of Antiquaries of Scotland*, vol. 142, 2013, pp. 371–412

Purkiss, Diane, *The Witch in History*, Oxford, Routledge, 1996

Rosen, Barbara, (ed.), *Witchcraft in England, 1558–1618*, The University of Massachusetts Press, 1991

Scot, Reginald, *The Discoverie of Witchcraft*, Dover, 1972

Serpell, James A., 'Guardian Spirits or Demonic Pets: The Concept of the Witch's Familiar in Early Modern England, 1530–1712', *The Animal/Human Boundary*, Rochester, NY, Rochester University Press, 2002

Shen, Qinna, 'Feminist Redemption of the Witch: Grimm and Michelet as Nineteenth-Century Models', *Focus on German Studies*, vol. 15, 2008, pp. 19–33

Smith, John B., 'Perchta the Belly-Slitter and her Kin: A View of Some Traditional Threatening Figures, Threats and Punishments', *Folklore*, vol. 115, no. 2, August 2004, pp. 167–86

Thwaite, Annie, 'What is a "witch bottle"? Assembling the textual evidence from early modern England', *Magic Ritual Witch*, vol. 15, no. 2, 2020, pp. 227–51

Valiente, Doreen, *The Rebirth of Witchcraft,* London, Robert Hale Ltd, 2007

Valiente, Doreen, and Jones, Evan John, *Witchcraft: A Tradition Renewed*, Custer, WA, Phoenix, 1990

Vukanovic, T.P., 'Witchcraft in the Central Balkans I: Characteristics of Witches', *Folklore,* vol. 100, no. 1, 1989, pp. 9–24

Vukanovic, T.P., 'Witchcraft in the Central Balkans II: Protection against Witches', *Folklore*, vol. 100, no. 2, 1989, pp. 221–36

Wilby, Emma, *The Visions of Isobel Gowdie: Magic, Witchcraft and Dark Shamanism in Seventeenth-Century Scotland*, Sussex, Sussex Academic Press, 2013

Willumsen, Liv Helene, 'Board Games, Dancing, and Lost Shoes: Ideas about witches' gatherings in the Finnmark witchcraft trials', *Demonology and Witch-hunting in Early Modern Europe*, Routledge, 2020, pp. 261–81

Willumsen, Liv Helene, 'Memorials to the Victims of the Witchcraft Trials: Orkney and Finnmark, Norway', *New Orkney Antiquarian Journal*, vol. 9, Orkney Heritage Society, 2020

Winsham, Willow, *Treasury of Folklore: Stars and Skies,* Batsford Books, 2023

Young, Simon, 'Witch in the Scales: Bible Weighing in England and America', *Magic, Ritual, and Witchcraft*, vol. 17, no. 1, summer 2022, pp. 106–35

Index

Adie, Lilias 167
Aelian 15
Africa 174–5
alewives 43–4
Alexandrian Wicca 132–3
Alkmene 15
Andersen, Hans Christian 23
Anna Goldi Museum 173
apples 150
Aradia 143
ash tree 109
Astor Place Riot 20
athame 124, 127

Baba Yaga 24, 27–9
Babylonian Code of Hammurabi 82
Baker, Diane 137–8
Bede 155
Befana, La 50–2
Beltane 77, 156–7
Bennett, Elizabth 98
Beth, Rae 140
Bible 41, 88–90
Bideford Witches 165, 167
Bishop, Bridget 86
bjara 34
bladders 111–13
Blåkulla 67–8, 73, 74
Blocksberg 67

blood 34–5, 36, 100, 105–6
'Book of Shadows' (Gardner) 122, 124, 139
Bourgeois, Louise 168
Bourne, Lois 125
Bowers, Roy 127
Brigid 143, 152–4
broomsticks 78–9, 104
Buckland, Raymond and Rosemary 125
Budapest, Z. 134
Buffy the Vampire Slayer (TV series) 16, 174
bullets 108
Burroughs, George 92, 169

Caddell, Christian 85
Cailleach 154
Candlemas 77, 154
Cardell, Charles 126, 139, 147
Caria, Turkey 13
Carr, Victoria 99
cats 34, 35, 95, 97
cauldrons 19
Centre for Pagan Studies 125, 130, 131
Cernunnos 146, 147
Chambers, Rachel 88
'Charge of the Goddess' 130
Charge of the Goddess (Valiente) 131
Charmed (TV series) 16

Charpentier, Catherine 74
Chelmsford witch trials 95, 97, 167
children 175
Christmas 45–8, 50–3, 76
'Cinderella' 26
Clarke, Bess 72
Cochrane, Robert 126–8, 130, 147
Compendium Maleficarum (Guazzo) 63
Cone of Power 161–2
Cooke, Mary 88
Cooper, Margaret 73
Cotta, John 107
The Country Justice (Dalton) 86
covens 124
Crane, Thomas Frederick 23
crossroads 14, 68
Crowley, Aleister 162
Crowley, Amado 162
Crowther, Patricia 125
Cullender, Rose 90, 91
Culliford, Frederick 112
curse tablets 14
Cutler, James 166

Daemonologie (James VI) 82
Dalton, Michael 86
dancing 65–6, 138
Danielecka, Krystyna Gajowa 31–2
Darling, Thomas 105
deities 13–16, 19–20, 120, 121, 127, 134–6, 137–8, 141–7, 159
Demeter 13–14, 154–5
Denny, Amy 90, 91
Deutsche Mythologie (Grimm) 155

Devil 67–8, 69, 71–4, 79, 101
dew 30–1
Diana 134–6
Dick, John 85
Discourse of Witchcraft (Perkins) 106
The Discoverie of Witchcraft (Scot) 103
dogs 15, 97–8, 101
Don, Natalie 171–2
Doreen Valiente Foundation 131
'Drawing Down the Moon' 124
'The Dun Cow' 23
Duncan, Geillis 69
Duncan, Helen 171–2

Easter 76, 77
Easter witches 68
Edelin, Guillaume 79
Edinburgh 167
Edwards, Susannah 167
Ellis, Gwen ferch 98
Enchantress 141–3
Encyclopedia Britannica 120
Eostre 155
Ephesus, Turkey 136
Epiphany 47–8, 50–2
equinoxes 77, 148, 154–5, 163
Essex Witch Hunts 72, 97, 98, 100, 167
Euripedes 14

'The Fair Angiola' 23, 25
fairy tales 10, 21–6, 99
familiars 86, 95–101
Farrar, Janet and Stewart 133
Farrar, Stewart 147

Fates 15, 19, 143
feasting 66
feminism 136, 137
ferns 108
Finnmark witch trials 65, 67, 73, 74, 76–7, 101, 167–8
fire 107, 150, 156, 157–8
flying ointments 63, 66, 79
folk tales 10, 21–6
Folklore Centre of Superstition and Witchcraft 125
Fox, Bridget 106
Francis, Elizabeth 97
Francis, Margaret 105
Frau Holle 48–50
Fraudulent Mediums Act (1951) 116
Frozen 174

Gale 15
Galinthias 15
Gardner, Gerald 120, 121–5, 129–30, 131, 161–2
garlic 108–9
Gascon, Mengeotte 71
ghosts 99
Giraldus Cambrensis 30–1
'The Girl Who Transformed Herself into a Hare' 38–40
The God of the Witches (Murray) 120
A Goddess Arrives (Gardner) 124
Goddess Festivals 134
goddesses 13–16, 19–20, 134–6, 137–8, 141–3, 153
'The Golden Bird' 24

Goldi, Anna 170
Good, Sarah 101
Gooderidge, Alice 92, 105
Gowdie, Isobel 41, 69, 74
Grant, William 106
Graves, Robert 143
Great Goddess 16, 141–3, 153
Greek mythology 13–15, 136
Green Man 146
Grimm, Jacob 155
Gryla 52–3
Guazzo, Francesco Maria 63

Hades 154–5
Halloween 77, 149–50
Hamilton, Margaret 42
The Hammer of Witches (Kramer) see The Hammer of Witches
Hammurabi, Code of 82
Hancocke, Elizabeth 93
'Hansel and Gretel' 21, 22, 23, 24
hares 30–1, 33, 34, 38–41
harvest festivals 159–60, 163
Harvey, Joan 105
hats 42–4
hawthorn 109–11
Haywood, Oliver 93–4
hearth chains 103–4
Hedge Witch – A Guide to Solitary Witchcraft (Rae) 140
hedge witches 139–40
The Hedge Witch's Way (Rae) 140
Hegeler, Hartmut 171
Hekabe/Hecuba 15–16

Hekate 13–16, 136, 143
Hekla (volcano) 67
Hell 14
Hera 15
Herakles 15
Hereditary Witchcraft 126, 128
Heria 51
Herne the Hunter 146–7
Herodotus 136
Hesiod 13
Hexenflug der Vaudoises 78
The History of the Devil (Thompson) 146
Holda 49
Holinshed's Chronicles 17
Holly King 144, 146, 151, 157
Homer 13–14
Hopkins, Matthew 72, 82, 85, 86, 87, 167
Horned God 120, 127, 143, 144–7, 151
horseshoes 103, 106
Howard, Raymond 126, 130, 147
Hunt, Alice 98
Hymn to Demeter (Homer) 13–14

Imbolc 152–4
imps 97, 98, 99–100
India 174–5
initiation 124, 132
Innes, John 85
invasion prevention 161–2
iron 102–4, 111
Isis 143
'Ivan Tsarevich, the Firebird, and the Grey Wolf' 27–9

Jacobs, Joseph 25
James VI of Scotland 82
Johnson, Elizabeth, Jr. 170
Johnson, Margaret 72
Jonsdatter, Margrette 73
'Jorinde and Joringel' 24

Kelly, Aidan 155, 163
Kemp, Ursula 97, 98, 100
Kent, Jane 111
Kerke, Anne 107
Kincaid, John 85
knives 104, 124, 127
Kramer, Heinrich 61

La-Feill Maire 160
la Rondelatte, Catherine 71
Lakeland, Mary 60
Lammas 77, 160, 161–2
LaPierre, Carrie 170
lating 149–50
Lauritsdatter, Anne 73
Le Champion des Dames (le Franc) 78
le Franc, Martin 78
lead 108
Leek, Sybil 126
Lillie, Marion 168
Lister, Thomas 91
Litha 157–8
Lloyd, Temperance 167
Lomonosov, Mikhail V. 27–9
Longridge Fell 149–50

Lord's Prayer recital 92
Lowes, John 87–8
Lughnasadh 159–60
Luna 136
Lyderhorn 67

Mabon 163
Macbeth (Shakespeare) 16, 17–20
Magi 51
Malleus Maleficarum (Kramer) 61–2, 107
Mather, Cotton 113
May Day 156–7
The Meaning of Witchcraft (Gardner) 124
Medea (Euripdes) 14
memorials and commemorations 165–8
Midsummer 144, 157–8
Midwinter 45–53, 151–2
milk-stealing 30–7
mistletoe 152
Moilean Maire 160
Moirai 15
Molland, Alice 167
moon 141, 163
Moore, Margaret 99
Mora witch trials 67
'The Morning Star and the Evening Star' 22
mountains 67
Murray, Margaret 119–20
Museo de las Brujas 173
Museum of Witchcraft 125, 140

Natural Magic (Valiente) 131
Nazis 161–2
Neopaganism 116, 120
Newman, Alice 100
Nilsdatter, Solve 65
Norse mythology 19
North Berwick witch trials 69, 74
Nurse, Rebecca 166
nuts 108, 150

Oak King 144–6, 151, 157
'The Old Witch' 25
Olufsdatter, Marrite 76–7
On the Characteristics of Animals (Aelian) 15
Operation Cone of Power 161–2
Operation Mistletoe 162
Osborne, Ruth and John 83
Ostara 154–5

Pagan Federation 130
Pagan Front 130
Palmer, Anne 98
pardons 169–73
Parris, Betty 94
parshell 150
Pedersdatter, Anne 67
Pendle witch trials 85, 91, 98, 171
Perchta 45–8
Percy Jackson book series (Riordan) 16
Perkins, William 106
persecution 174–5 see also witch trials
Persephone 14, 154–5, 163
Pilecka, Dorotea 31–2

pins 104, 105, 106, 111
plants 108–11, 152
Pliny the Elder 102
Potter, Joan 99–100
Powell, Margaret 98
Practical Magic (film, 1998) 16
Prentice, Joan 100
Preston, Jennet 91
pricking 84–5
protection from bewitchment 102–13, 150
Psychic News 127

Qabalah 132
Quakers 43

'Rapunzel' 24–5
Rasmusdatter, Marette 101
The Rebirth of Witchcraft (Valiente) 131
Reclaiming Tradition 137
Remembering the Accused Witches of Scotland (RAWS) 171–2
Riordan, Rick 16
rituals 124, 132–3, 138, 161–2
The Robert Cochrane Letters (Cochrane) 128
The Roebuck in the Thicket (Cochrane) 128
rowan tree 109

Sabbaths 63–70, 76
Sabbats 148
Sabrina the Teenage Witch 174

Salem witch trials 70, 73, 86, 94, 101, 113, 166, 169–70, 173, 174
Samhain 16, 149–50
Sampson, Agnes 69
Samuel, Alice 86, 92, 106
Sanders, Alex and Maxine 132–3
Scot, Reginald 103
scratching a witch 104, 105–6
seasons 121, 140, 141, 144, 148–60, 163
Selene 136
Shakespeare, William 16, 17–20
shape-shifting 15, 23, 30, 38–41, 98
'The Shot Hare' 40–1
Sibley, Mary 94
Simos, Miriam 137–8
sleep deprivation 86–8
Smith, Maggie 166
Smith, Mary 93
snakkur 36
The Snow Queen 21
snowdrops 153
solstices 144–6, 148, 151–2, 157–8
Spanish Armada 161–2
Spanish Inquisition 62
Spellcraft for Hedge Witches (Rae) 140
spinning 47, 48–9
The Spiral Dance (Starhawk) 137
Sprenger, Jakob 61
St Brigid 152–4
St John's Eve 76–7, 158
St John's nuts 108
St Thomas's Day Eve 109
St Walpurga's Eve 77
stang 127

Starhawk 137–8
Stearne, John 85, 86
Stonehenge 158
storytelling heritage 10–12
Stregheria 147
Strenia 51
Sturgeon, Nicola 171–2
Sutton, Mary and Mother 97
swimming a witch 80–3
sympathetic magic 94, 111

Tailtiu 159
teats 86, 100
Thanksgiving 163
theatre 20, 21
Theogony (Hesiod) 13
Thompson, R. Lowe 146
Thorn, Ann 106
thorns 109–11
'The Three Golden Hairs' 24
Tiepel, Christine 66
tilberi 36–7
toads 95
touch test 90–1
tourism 173–4
Traditional Witchcraft 126, 128, 130–1, 143, 147
transformations 15, 23, 30, 38–41, 98
transitions 16, 149
trees 108–11, 152
Trembles, Mary 167
Triple Goddess 14, 127, 136, 141–3, 153
troll cats 34–6

trolls 52
trows 149
'The Twelve Wild Ducks' 23

Underworld 14, 154–5
Unknown God 127

Valiente, Doreen 122, 125, 128, 129–31, 140, 147
'Vasilisa the Beautiful' 27
Virgil 14
volcanoes 67

Wagg, Anne 106
waking as torture 86–7
walking as torture 87–8
Wall, Maggie 168
Wallis, Joan 98
walnuts 108
Walpurgis Nacht 77
Waterhouse, Agnes 95, 97, 98
Wayside Witches 140
weighing a witch 88–90
Weird Sisters 19–20
wells 153–4
Wenham, Jane 90–1, 92, 106
West, Rebecca 72
Wheel of the Year 121, 148–60, 163
'The White Dove' 23–4
'The White Duck' 23
White Goddess 143
White Shrovetide 108–9
Whittier, John Greenleaf 166
Whittle, Ann 98
Wicca see also Gardner, Gerald; Great

Goddess; Horned God; Valiente, Doreen

Alexandrian Wicca 132–3
Dianic Wicca 134–6
Hekabe/Hecuba 16
Margaret Murray 120
Reclaiming Tradition 137–8
The Wiccan Path (Rae) 140
Wiccan Rede 129, 130
Wilby, Emma 70
'The Wild Swans' 23
Wild Woman 141–3
Williams, Abigail 94
Williamson, Cecil 125, 140
Wilson, Joseph 128
Wilson, Monique 125
'Witch as Hare' 40
witch bottles 111–13
witch cakes 93–4
Witch Camps 138
The Witch-Cult in Western Europe (Murray) 119–20
'The Witch in the Stone Boat' 24
'The Witch of the Ardennes' 26
witch trials
Bideford 167
Chelmsford 95, 97, 167
Essex 72, 97, 98, 100, 167
execution methods 60
Finnmark 65, 67, 73, 74, 76–7, 101, 167–8
Malleus Maleficarum (Kramer) 61–2
memorials and commemorations 165–8
Mora 67

North Berwick 69, 74
number executed 56
pardons 169–73
Pendle 85, 91, 98, 171
proof methods 80–94
Salem 70, 73, 86, 94, 101, 113, 166, 169–70, 173, 174
women 59
Witchcraft Act (1604) 97
Witchcraft for Tomorrow (Valiente) 131
Witchcraft Research Association 130
Witchcraft Research Centre 140
Witchcraft Today (Gardner) 124
Witches of Scotland 171–2
'Witches of Subeshi' 44
Witches' Well, Edinburgh 167
Witchfinder General see Hopkins, Matthew
WitchTok 117
The Wizard of Oz 42
women 21, 134–6
Women's Spirituality Forum 134
World War II 161–2
Wyard, Margaret 73
Wyrd 19

Yule 144, 151–2
Yule Cat and Yule Lads 53

Zeus 13, 15, 154–5
Zumthor, Peter 168

First published in the United Kingdom
in 2025 by
Batsford
43 Great Ormond Street
London
WC1N 3HZ

An imprint of B. T. Batsford Holdings Limited

Copyright © B. T. Batsford Ltd, 2025
Text copyright © Willow Winsham, 2025
Illustrations by Katie Ponder

All rights reserved. No part of this publication may be copied, displayed, extracted, reproduced, utilized, stored in a retrieval system or transmitted in any form or by any means, electronic, mechanical or otherwise including but not limited to photocopying, recording, or scanning without the prior written permission of the publishers.

ISBN 9781849949064

A CIP catalogue record for this book is available from the British Library.

10 9 8 7 6 5 4 3 2

Reproduction by Mission Productions, Hong Kong
Printed by Elma Basim, Turkey

This book can be ordered direct from the publisher at www.batsfordbooks.com, or try your local bookshop.

Distributed throughout the UK and Europe by Abrams & Chronicle Books, 1 West Smithfield, London EC1A 9JU and 57 rue Gaston Tessier, 75166 Paris, France

www.abramsandchronicle.co.uk
info@abramsandchronicle.co.uk